all the best

The best wine for **pizza**. The best wine to **get the party started**. The best wine for **BBQ'd burgers**. The best wine for **chilling out**. The best wine for **steak**. The best wine **under ten dollars**. The best wine for **after work**. The best wine for **romance**. The best **local wine**. The best wine to **beat the heat**. The best wine for the **novice**. The best wine for **everyday meals**. The best **nice** wine. The best **wild** wine. The best **Shiraz**. The best seducers. **The best wine book.**

to all those who like wine

. . . and to all those who would like to

Written, produced and published by Billy Munnelly

Designed by Kato Wake

Printed by Commercial Printers in Stratford, Ontario

ISBN 0-9693717-4-8

Special thanks to 50 really good BEST BOTTLES wineletter subscribers and
to all those who were with us on September 22, 2002

Additional copies available for $24.95 [tax and postage included] from
BILLY'S BEST BOTTLES
589 Markham Street
Toronto Ontario
M6G 2L7

P 416 530 1545
F 415 539 1575
E info@billysbestbottles.com

www.billysbestbottles.com

Distributed to the retail trade by WHITECAP BOOKS, Vancouver 604.980.9852

THE 13th EDITION OF

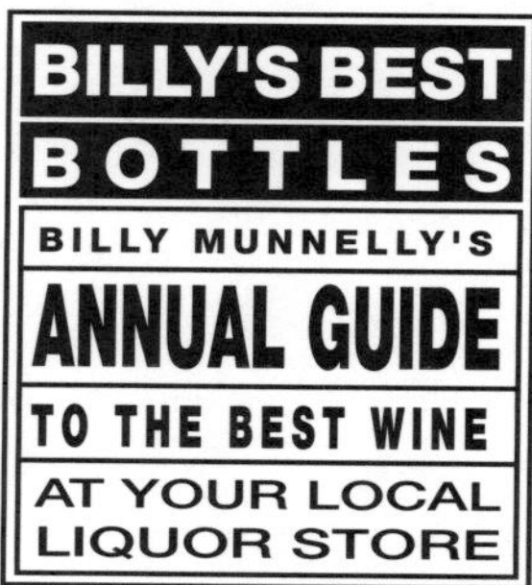

NOT ONLY THE **BEST** WINES . . . BUT HOW TO **USE** THEM

MADE IN ONTARIO BUT GOOD FOR ALL OTHER CANADIAN PROVINCES.

While this book recommends the best wines offered in Ontario, many of them are available in other provinces. Simply supply the CSPC code number listed after the name of each wine in this book and your store will be able to tell you if the wine is available or not.

This year's good wine news is that the quality keeps getting better while prices remain reasonable. Almost half of my recommendations are in the under ten dollars price bracket. It's a buyers market for sure as new wineries open every day and production exceeds demand. I'm trying as hard as I can and I'm sure your thirst will increase once you've sampled everything in this book.

Every year I spend over $10,000 on wine. That's cash out of my pocket. I could call up wine importers and scrounge free samples, but if I'm going to review wines properly and without bias, it's important that I pay my own way. Because I buy and taste every wine offered, I get to know how one compares with the next, and whether or not a bottle is

worth the money. I am a paying costumer, just like you. There are just over 100 picks, in my book, which is about ten percent of what's offered – that seems to be the average ratio of good to bland in most things today.

For a wine buying book to be useful I think that it must offer more than just a list of what to buy – it must also advise on when to drink the wines. Wine is not just a taste-with-tongue experience – it involves mood and situation. It's a much a feeling as it is a flavour. Wine works best when it has the right feeling for the moment and mood. That is why I start each page with the question of mood. When you match wine and mood you create good times.

My book is small because I do not believe you need to know all the facts about each wine – where it was produced, who made it, what type of grapes were used, etc.. My main interest is how a wine tastes and feels, and how it might fit into our lives.

Even Mateus Rosé is tasting good. Start celebrating. Take this book along to the store and start shopping. Cheers!

Billy Munnelly

P.S. Check out my WINE SPECTRUM chart on page 17. It's what every wine lover ever wanted. Makes the subject a lot easier to understand.

a few things about this book

This book will help you choose the best wine without spending a lot of time and money. This book is for people who enjoy variety in their drinking and are open to new experiences. This book is especially useful for the beginner, or for anyone who wants quick answers on which wine to buy. This book is about getting the most out of wines by drinking them in the context for which they are intended. This book will take you on a guided tour of your local liquor store, pointing out the best wines in each style.

Most wine books celebrate the high and mighty of the wine world. My focus is on the middle ground, the good everyday, the trooper, the Toyota. Wines to get you through the week – and take you on the occasional trip. Wines to drink rather than worship.

what's a good wine?

Before you ask what's good

you need to ask yourself **'what am I in the mood for?'**

All my selections in this book are arranged by mood.
Simply match your mood with the wines and you're all set.

it's not about price

Don't fall for expensive or prestigious wines. They can be impressive in much the same way as the great cathedrals of Europe. A wow for sure, but their grandeur is overwhelming and intimidating. They do not create a huge desire to return. Over the years I have noticed that we have the best relationships with places and pleasures that are not so big, important or grand. We like to be able to work fun into life and that happens more readily when we take the low road. The back street café over the fancy joint. I drink the wines in this book not just because they are good value, but because they give me the best times.

Wine works according to a setting and a specific moment. Great wine experiences do not require a great wine – just one that's right for the context.

Wine is not about prestige . . . it is about pleasure.

what if there was a system

to help you choose the right wine, every time

imagine how good it would feel

I've always felt that the difficulty with wine has been that it's poorly defined. Stores and restaurants offer wine by country, price or grape variety, but this does not tell people what to expect. Information about places, grapes, history and vintages do nothing to help us choose the right bottle to put on the table. People can select the kind of music they want because the subject has well-defined categories – the per son looking for opera never buys rock and roll by mistake.

The **WINE SPECTRUM CHART** that you'll find on the next page is my way of categorizing wine. It shows where wines fit in relation to each other, and it shows where they might fit into our lives. It's what the science world might call a 'breakthrough' in wine understanding – explaining it all in one chart. Everything you need in one formula.

Almost every decision made in life marks a spot on a spectrum of choices. Only by knowing what your choices are can you make a selection. My WINE SPECTRUM shows you what's available in the wine world, and tells you where you are once you choose. Where to go next is an easy decision because you know where you've been. Having a spectrum is like having a road map – something that helps you get where you want to be. Or helps you go elsewhere without getting lost.

The spectrum categories evolved through an understanding of our basic wine needs: something to drink with everyday meals [MEDIUM], something for richer times and foods [RICH], and something to refresh or to get an event started [FRESH]. We need total of 6 wines to cover these three needs because of the possibility of a red or whit selection. All wines chosen for this book are identified by their category – a 'when t drink it' guide. Take a minute to read the guide pages at the beginning of each category. Consider having a stock of all 6 categories on hand and you will be prepared for an mood or event.

P.S. Sweet and fortified wines are in a section called 'FRINGE' which you'll find after th 6 main category picks.

experience contrast

it's the best way to learn

TAKE THE TEST!

Get a few friends together to split the cost and share in the experience. Plan some food for after. Buy a bottle of each of the following:

FRESH WHITE: SOGRAPE VINHO VERDE 'GAZELA', Portugal [page 35]

RICH WHITE: SANTA RITA 2000 CHARDONNAY 'RESERVA', Chile [page 87]

MEDIUM WHITE: HENRY OF PELHAM 2001 CHARDONNAY 'NON-OAKED', Ontario [page 53]

Experience the wines in the above order.

It's easier to get a sense of different wine styles when you experience them side by side. The uplifting nature of a FRESH WHITE and the mellow feeling of a RICH WHITE register more clearly when contrasted with each other. The different uses of the two styles become very obvious. As does the appeal of wines in the mid-range. Biggest is not always the best.

the 100 best wines

and when to drink them

fresh white

To refresh + stimulate. To quench your thirst.

THIRST QUENCHERS

WHITE WINES THAT ARE SIMPLE, FRESH AND A LITTLE JOLTING.

FOOD PAIRING: antipasti, sushi, oysters, Asian foods, goat cheese, smoked salmon.

Refreshing wines to have before a meal, whenever you are thirsty, or with 'fresh' appetizers. These wines are light on their feet and full of energy. They are the equivalent of the lively music you'd play to get the party started. Assertive, yet simple.

WATCHPOINT: Don't overdo FRESH wines.The tartness can get annoying after a few glasses, like playing the same CD for an entire night. Refrigerated open bottles will keep well for 3 to 4 days.

getting started

the first glass

In the mood for an opening act.

What's a good wine to get the party or the evening started? A lively, sparkling wine, of course. Often the host will think of serving something nice up front – but liveliness beats niceness if you want your event to get off the ground. That first glass should deliver a lift. A shot of energy.

One of the delights in today's wine world is the availability of wonderful bubbly at an everyday price. There is no reason why our evenings shouldn't start with glasses of tingling, fresh, sparkling wine.

service

Serve well-chilled in a simple narrow glass tumbler, or use a Champagne flute if you wish.

I wouldn't dream of kicking off a party without **PROSECCO DI VALDOBBIADENE 2001 BRUT, Italy** [#340570 $11.60]. This Italian fizz is the most light-hearted sparkling wine in the world. It always produces a smile. Prosecco is drunk young because lightness and playfulness are its nature. The French have created an aura of luxury around Champagne, but the Italians believe that sparkling wine should be an everyday drink, at an everyday price.

Australia also believes in having fun with sparkling wine. **DEAKIN ESTATE BRUT** [#876264 $11.95] and **JACOB'S CREEK BRUT CUVEÉ CHARDONNAY/PINOT NOIR** [#562991 $13.25] are two super, clean-cut, party starter or aperitif wines.

P.S. See FRINGE section for more sparkling wine selections.

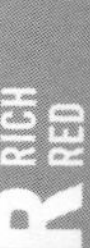

an after work pick-me-up

happy hour wine

In the mood for an after work refresher.

Something tangy and dry works best. I favour lighthearted wines – crisp and clean over rich and heavy. Save flavour and character for later in the evening. This is not the time to tax your attention or your energy. Refreshers put an end to the cares of the day and create the mood for supper.

service

Serve well-chilled in a small glass tumbler or medium-sized wine glass. One or two glasses is usually enough, after that this style of wine becomes boring.

TYRRELL'S 2001 'LONG FLAT' WHITE, Australia [#183715 $9.90] is a high voltage, herbaceous

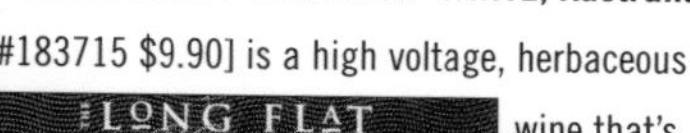

wine that's sure to energize the most jaded palate. Slimmer and more tangy than what we have come to expect from Australia.

Old favourite, **TORRES 2000 VINA SOL, Spain** [#28035 $9.45] is still one of the best refreshers to be had. It tingles in the mouth with lovely citrus and mineral zest.

Fans of livewire Sauvignon Blanc will welcome a glass of **PHILIPPE DE ROTHSCHILD 2001 SAUVIGNON BLANC, VDP D'OC, France** [#407536 $9.50]. Not for the timid.

New Zealand's **STONELEIGH 2001 RIESLING** [#527713 $11.95] has Granny Smith apple crunch and purity. Lime flavours add to the tingle.

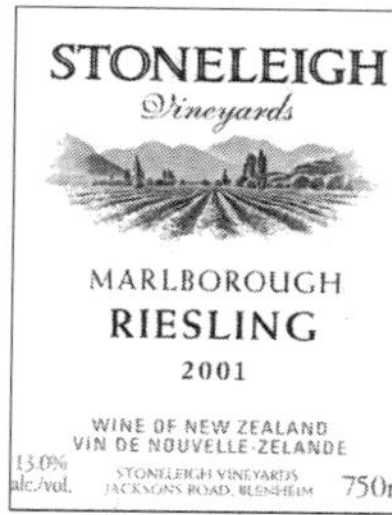

If you'd like to know what they drink after work in **South Africa**, try **KWV 2002 CHENIN BLANC** [#18689 $7.00]. It's powerfully thirst quenching – and inexpensive.

P.S. See next page for more selections in this category.

more after work refreshers

happy hour wine

In the mood for an after work refresher.

Ontario Dry Riesling is one of the best refreshers in the world. It's our great contributio to the world of wine. Try this test. Chill any of the wines on the opposite page and d something to work up a thirst. Now try the wine. I guarantee it will be uplifting. It wi hit the spot.

service

The live wire nature of Dry Riesling is great for one or three glasses, but after that, you need to switch to a calmer, more nourishing wine. Raw oysters, smoked salmon, and seafood appetizers are good food partners for Dry Riesling. Glass tumblers or medium-sized glasses are best.

ENRY OF PELHAM 2001 DRY RIESLING, #268375 $10.95], **CAVE SPRING 2000 DRY IESLING** [#233635 $10.95], **INNISKILLIN 2001 IESLING** [#83790 $9.95], and **JACKSON-RIGGS 2001 DRY RIESLING** [#526277 $9.45] re the Ontario champions of Dry Riesling.

Mineral and citrus flavours give these wines an energizing 'spa' quality – the cool stream in the shade of the woods. Never be without an open bottle in the fridge.

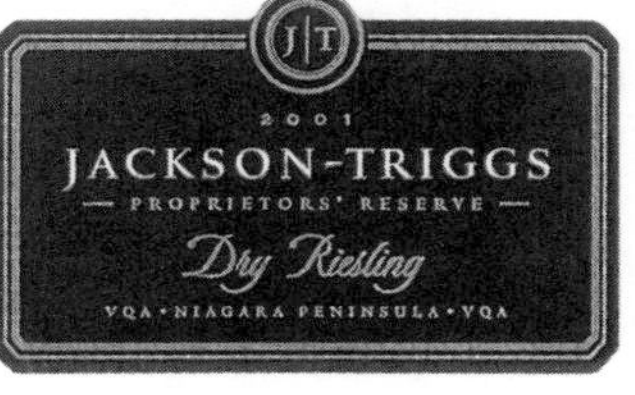

P.S. If you can handle really dry whites add **VINELAND 2000 DRY RIESLING** [#167551 $9.95] to the list.

P.S.S. There are more local Rieslings in the MEDIUM WHITES section of this book.

dry, but not too dry

yummy and refreshing

In the mood for a white wine that is slightly sweet but still refreshingly dry.

Honest – it is possible to find a white wine with sweet, fruit flavours that is also refreshingly dry. Wines made from Gewurztraminer or Muscat grapes often have this qualit They are called the aromatic family of wines. Try my selections and you'll see what mean. I've seen many a non-drinker lose their self-control after a sip or two c Gewurztraminer.

The hit of flavour in aromatic wines sedates the palate so we tend not to gulp them a quickly as we might bone dry wines. Something to keep in mind if your drinking start long before your eating.

service

Serve well chilled. You could echo the fun of these wines by serving them in odd-shaped glasses.

CHATEAU BONNET 2001 BORDEAUX, France [#83709 $12.95] continues to be one of the world's great, fun whites. A must for parties or Sunday brunch. Works equally well for both the novice and the seasoned wino.

Hungary's contribution to this category is a great value called **DUNAVAR 2000 MUSCAT** [#565812 $6.95]. It delivers a lot of flavour and tartness. An exciting cocktail-hour wine or partner for foods in a cream sauce.

Another treat in this category is **ARESTI 2001 GEWURZTRAMINER 'MONTEMAR', Chile** [#605691 $9.10]. It's a delicious combo of zest and flavour. Sip anytime. Great for lazy Sundays.

Last, but not least, is the light, lean, brisk **JACKSON-TRIGGS 2001 GEWURZTRAMINER 'BLACK LABEL', Ontario** [#526269 $9.95]. It has a great sense of fun, so enjoy often.

a good everyday dry wine

no need for an occasion

In the mood for good, everyday, refreshing wine.

Good, plain, white wine is like a plain white t-shirt. You cannot explain what's good about it, but it feels right. The following wines make a fresh statement in a mild-mannered, friendly way. They are good 'anytime' refreshers.

service

Serve well chilled in a tumbler or medium-sized glass.

CAVE SPRING 2000 AUXEROIS/PINOT BLANC, Ontario [#500975 $10.95] tastes a lot like house wine at a bistro in France. Simple but just right.

PELEE ISLAND 2001 PINOT GRIS, Ontario [#326413 $9.95] seems plain at first, but by the second glass you'll discover its subtle charm.

DUNAVAR 2001 PINOT BLANC, Hungary [#565820 $6.95] is zesty and quite delicious. Fun to drink and, at this price, it's fun to buy too.

ANTINORI 2001 ORVIETO CLASSICO 'CAMPOGRANDE', Italy [#18838 $9.95] continues to shine in this 'simple but enjoyable' category. Feels modern and uplifting.

beat the heat

wines to sip on the dock

In the mood for quenching your thirst on a hot, summer day.

Summer days are better with VINHO VERDE wine. That may sound like a commercial bu it's the truth. Vinho Verde is a peasant wine from the north of Portugal that is slightl spritzy, keenly tart and as pure as spring water. You can guzzle it freely because it ha 50% less alcohol than the average Chardonnay. There's no better summer wine for day time and early evening drinking. You can keep it going into supper with salad or seafoo appetizers, but the wine's strength is its ability to tackle the daytime heat.

service

Serve Vinho Verde icy cold in glasses. No need for stemware.

SOGRAPE VINHO VERDE 'GAZELA', Portugal [#131432 $7.10] is a great expression of the pure, fresh, lighthearted quality of Vinho Verde.

One gulp and you feel refreshed. More fun than Perrier but sort of similar in feeling.

AVELEDA 2001 VINHO VERDE, Portugal [#5322 $7.05] is quite fizzy and less tart so

it would be a real crowd-pleaser. Think of it as summer Champagne, your daily tonic, your splash of fun. If it were an apple it would be Golden Delicious, whereas the 'GAZELA' would be a Granny Smith.

P.S. The 'verde' part of the name refers to the fact that the grapes were picked while still green, which accounts for the wine's refreshing tartness and low alcohol.

MEZZA CORONA 2001 PINOT GRIGIO, Italy [#302380 $11.35] is from Italy's Apline region and has the same bracing freshness as Vinho Verde. Very pure and spring-like. Gets you going.

to start a special occasion

the classy cocktail

In the mood for celebrating something special!

It is not well known that most champagnes belong to the fresh category of wines Champagnes labeled Brut are particularly austere, low flavoured and jolting. They ar not for everyone. But if you're a fan, use these wines to toast friends or an occasion, or si them before a meal. Champagne's glamorous aura shines brightest as an opening act

service

Serve Champagne cold and use a stemmed or 'fluted' glass. Open carefully, keeping the bottle angled at 4 and pointing it away from valued friends and possessions. Pour slowly so the foam has time to settle.

POL ROGER BRUT CHAMPAGNE, France

[#51953 $44.95] is austere but deliciously teasing – the classic aperitif.

NICOLAS FEUILLATE BRUT CHAMPAGNE, France

[#537605 $39.85] is equally good at this job, a real live wire. Bold, tart and uplifting.

PIPER HEIDSIECK BRUT CHAMPAGNE, France

[#361626 $42.95] is high spirited with a light-hearted feeling. Certainly of the cocktail spirit.

P.S. See FRINGE section for more sparkling wines.

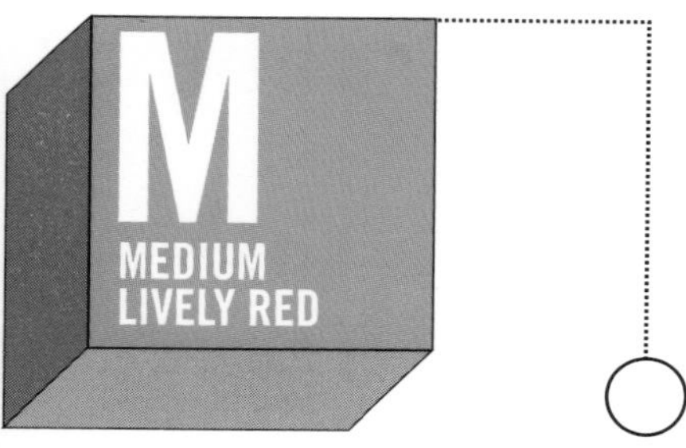

medium lively red

Wines in the mid-range to celebrate the everyday.

FOR LIGHTER EVERYDAY MEALS

THESE WINES FEEL FRESHER AND LIVELIER THAN ALL OTHER REDS – THEY LEAN TOWARDS THE FRESHER SIDE OF MEDIUM. SERVE LIGHTLY CHILLED.

FOOD PAIRING: pizza, roast chicken, BBQ's, 'red' pasta, burgers, grilled salmon.

These are the wines that sit on the dinner table in the homes of the old wine countries, and on the tables in bistros, trattorias and tavernas. They're about sociability + aiding digestion. Some days they will seem heavenly, and other times just good company.

WATCHPOINT: Drink and enjoy all MEDIUM wines without too much fuss. It is essential to lightly chill these wines. Refrigerated open bottles will keep well for 3 to 4 days.

red, but really refreshing

fun, drink-me-quick reds

In the mood for red wine for lively times – everyday meals, picnics in the park or parties.

How can red wine be refreshing, you ask? The production technique for some reds, such as Beaujolais [made from the Gamay grape], results in wine with the characteristics of a white. So they are intended to be chilled [lightly] and gulped. I'll tell ya, once you've had a few cool glasses of a fresh red you may never go back to white wines.

Summer is the season for these wines because they complement almost all foods of that season and bring cheer to any event, but I include chilled, fresh reds at parties all year round because of their lighthearted nature.

One of the changes I'd like to see in the wine world would be the use of clear glass bottles for light, refreshing reds. It's a shame to hide these cheerful wines in serious-looking dark bottles.

service

Lightly chill and serve in tumblers or moderate-sized glasses.

CAVE SPRING 2000 GAMAY, Ontario [#228569 $11.95] is certainly lively and cheerful. It really shines in the picnic, lunch, appetizer, or party role. Think of it as the fun hour – a little wine, a little food and a lot of laughs. Chill lightly.

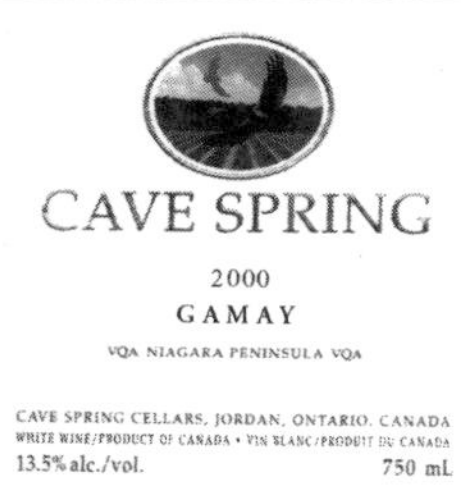

GEORGES DUBOEUF 2001 BEAUJOLAIS-VILLAGES, France [#122077 $12.95] is charming and dangerously drinkable. Very French café*ish*. Great stuff for everyday drinking or to pour for a party. Chill lightly.

THORIN 2001 COTES DU VENTOUX 'GRAND RESERVE DE CHALLIERES', France [#331090 $8.90] is made by the same process as Beaujolais. Bright, juicy flavours are nicely edged with a refreshing bite. There's a shine and a vitality that says 'enjoy'. I bet you will. Everyday red wines don't get much better.

LAMBERTI 2001 VALPOLICELLA 'SANTEPIETRE', Italy [#560508 $10.45] could hardly be more lively. A fruity, bright, refreshing wine that feels light and suggests daytime or early evening drinking. A party refresher for sure.

refreshing and charming

a couple of local acts worth catching

In the mood for yummy red wine that's not fancy or rich. Lighthearted wine to have with burgers, chicken or grilled salmon.

Lighthearted and charming is a combination that you may not be familiar with but it part of the appeal of Pinot Noir wine. I'm sure you'll become a fan once you taste the pair on the next page. Pinot Noir is a great seducer.

service

Lightly chill and drink from medium-sized glasses.

INNISKILLIN 2001 PINOT NOIR, Ontario [#261099 $12.95] delivers a rush of ripe, sweet berry and country market flavours followed by a gentle, seductive touch. The charm and sensual nature of Pinot for sure. But you don't need to wait for a sexy mood – this is fun wine to slosh with a burger, ribs or a Mexican supper. The beauty of Pinot is that it fits in anywhere. Lightly chilled, of course. This would also be a popular party drink.

Although the colour of **MISSION HILL 2000 PINOT NOIR 'BIN 99', Okanagan Valley, B.C.** [#118844 $12.95] is barely darker than Rosé, and the first impression is of a lighthearted wine, it has what I call the oriental carpet or Marrakech quality – a Moroccan sultry, spicy, sexy aura. Pinot is, after all, for people who want to take a trip. Spice up your favourite food – grilled salmon or chicken with cumin would be great – and take off. Flying was never more fun or affordable. Also a great party drink. Chilled, of course.

best partners for pizza

Italian exuberance

In the mood for lively red wine to partner with pizza or pasta in tomato sauce.

You would never have to ask for a lively red in an Italian café. It's usually the only kin they serve. Italian food is exuberant and so are Italian wines. They refresh and the encourage lighthearted, fun times. The lesson to learn from Italy is to keep wine sim ple but enjoy it often. At least once a day.

service

Lightly chill these wines and serve in tumblers or medium-sized glasses.

BERSANO 2000 BARBERA D'ASTI 'COSTALUNGA', Italy [#348680 $10.95] has the vibrant, drink-me-quick quality of Beaujolais. Fresh and lighthearted – it's perfect for everyday times and meals. And any outdoor summer event.

ROCCA DELLE MACIE 2001 CHIANTI 'VERNAIOLO', Italy [#269589 $9.95] is a spirited, dynamic, young Chianti, at a decent price. Packed with gusto, it's mighty refreshing, and tangy enough to get you through the biggest pizza, bowl of pasta or platter of bruschetta.

SPINELLI 2001 MONTEPULCIANO D'ABRUZZO 'QUARTANA', Italy [#454629 $6.45] feels like it never left Italy. The spirited, earthy character will make your pizza taste 'more' Italian.

CANTINA TOLLO 2001 MONTEPULCIANO D'ABRUZZO 'ROCCA VENTOSA', Italy [#428532 $6.50] has the frank, no-nonsense quality that we enjoy in friends. It's tasty, lively and as good-as-it-needs-to-be. One of the world's great values in red wine.

minor merlots

Italian style

In the mood for lighthearted, everyday red – at a lighthearted pric

There are many kinds of Merlot. The rich and expensive variety is the most well know but Italy produces a light style that's fun to drink with everyday meals – Merlots th work equally well with pizza or hamburgers.

service

Lightly chill these wines and serve in tumblers or medium-sized glasses.

CESARI 2001 MERLOT DELLE VENEZIE, Italy [#572453 $6.50] has delicious, plummy-sweet flavours, a bright 'n cheerful personality and a refreshing tang. Hard to beat for pleasant house wine. Chill a notch.

LAMBERTI 2001 MERLOT DELLE VENEZIE 'SANTEPIETRE', Italy [#594143 $9.95] is probably one of the freshest and most light-hearted Merlot's you'll ever taste. Think fruity red – think lightly chilled – and hot, juicy burgers coming off the BBQ. Fun, fun, fun.

real men drink dry rosé

think pink for summer

In the mood for wines for outdoor summer meals, picnics or parties

North Americans don't take Rosé seriously because it is associated with Blush – th 'soda pop' wine. Travel to Spain or the south of France, however, and we discover a dif ferent kind of Rosé – one with serious credentials – being enjoyed on a daily basis. Eve the men drink it.

Any food that you'd want to eat outdoors would be the right partner for Rosé: antipast dishes, appetizers, salads of all kinds and fish or seafood. Salmon with Rosé is not onl a match of pretty colours but also of spirits. While Rosé wines may give the impressio of being lighthearted, many are deliberately high in alcohol in order to handle the o and garlic of Mediterranean foods such as paella or couscous. And don't be afraid of little hot spice. Rosé has Latin blood.

Buy a selection and have a few bottles open. Rosé looks more attractive in a grou brightening the tabletop in the same way that flowers do.

service

Chill as you would with whites, but if you're having Rosé with meals, leave the bottle out of the ice. It w develop more flavours as it warms up. Consider tumblers instead of stemware for parties and informal mea

nore this category till the summer because at's when the Board puts out its great array Rosé wines. You'll find lots to choose from. have found that **Spanish Rosés** have been the est all-rounders.

south of France Rosé at's always available, **AN JEAN 2001 ROSÉ RAH, VDP D'OC** 355347 $8.65] is od refreshment, while e Provence wines sually at Vintages in mmer] have the stuff- g for mealtimes.

VE SPRING and **HENRY OF PELHAM** have en producing very good local efforts in a edium style.

Italian Rosés tend to be lighthearted – great hot weather refreshment.

SOGRAPE 'MATEUS ROSÉ', Portugal [#166 $7.40] has been reborn in a drier style and I suggest that you give it another chance. This is no longer the frivolous stuff of old, but a decent everyday refresher or party drink. You might welcome the low alcohol for daytime tippling. A slight spritz adds to the fun and the smart new package is graceful enough for the fanciest condo. Time to ditch the Blush and get back to Mateus.

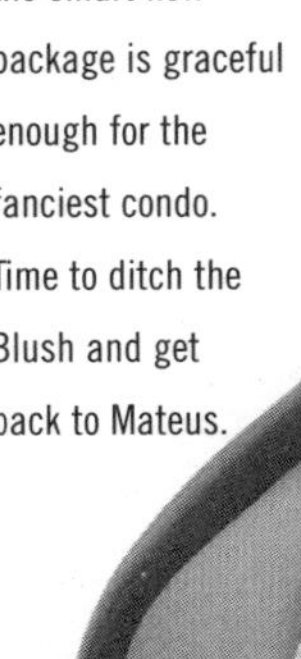

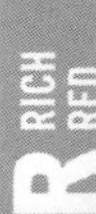

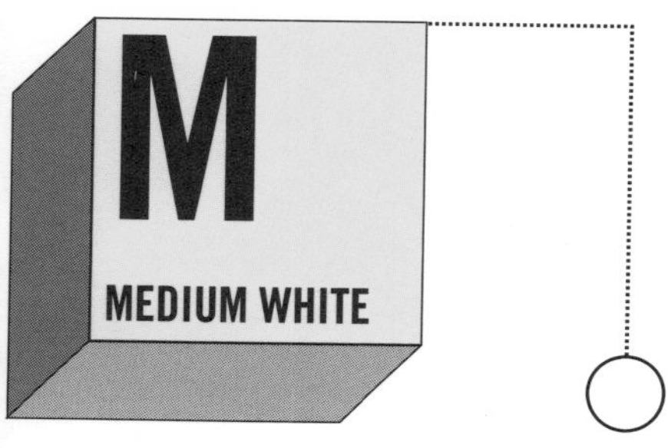

medium white

Wines in the mid-range to celebrate the everyday.

FOR EVERYDAY MEALS

WINES THAT ARE NOT TOO LIGHT, NOT TOO RICH – JUST MEDIUM!

FOOD PAIRING: white meats, chicken, 'white' pasta, fish, seafood, egg dishes.

These are the wines that sit on the dinner table in the homes of the old wine countries, and on the tables in bistros, trattorias and tavernas. They're about sociability + aiding digestion. Some days they will seem heavenly, and other times just good company.

WATCHPOINT: Drink and enjoy all MEDIUM wines without too much fuss. Refrigerated open bottles will keep well for 3 to 4 days.

good for everyday meals

the locals

In the mood for chicken, pork, seafood or pasta in a cream sauce.

Chardonnay has become synonymous with fullness and richness but this is not always so. Some Chardonnays are more everyday, more moderate. The ones here would be right at home with your weeknight supper.

Local winemakers have good reason to be proud of what they have achieved with this grape. What's particularly pleasing to me is the quality of the $10 to $12 wines. They are on par with the best imports.

service

Have your first glass well chilled and refreshing, but then let the wine warm up a bit to bring out the flavours. Use medium-sized glasses.

JACKSON-TRIGGS 2001 CHARDONNAY, Ontario [#526251 $10.45] has the tropical fruit flavours, the glamour and the zest that make Chards so popular. I particularly like this wine's level of refreshment – it helps to carry the flavour.

CHATEAU DES CHARMES 2001 CHARDONNAY ESTATE, Ontario [#81653 $12.95] is wonderfully invigorating at first and then it begs for food. Very French.

HENRY OF PELHAM 2001 CHARDONNAY 'NON-OAKED', Ontario [#291211 $10.95] is fun, flavourful and refreshing. The perfect house wine. A local hero for sure.

INNISKILLIN 2000 CHARDONNAY 'RESERVE', Ontario [#317768 $12.95] is quite tangy. A bold, citrusy character suggests an aperitif, but there is an earthy quality too that will marry well with highly seasoned grilled chicken or seafood.

good for everyday meals

the imports

In the mood for chicken, pork, seafood or pasta in a cream sauce.

France is well known for its famous and expensive wines but recently it has also becom quite good at producing quality, everyday wines. The packaging still looks traditional bu the wines are thoroughly modern.

service

Have your first glass well chilled and refreshing, but then let the wine warm up a bit to bring out the flavours. Use medium -sized glasses.

ROTHSCHILD 2001 CHARDONNAY VDP D'OC, France [#407528 $9.95] is a lovely, pure expression of the grape, with just enough glamour to make it special. Satisfies without tiring. Good anytime.

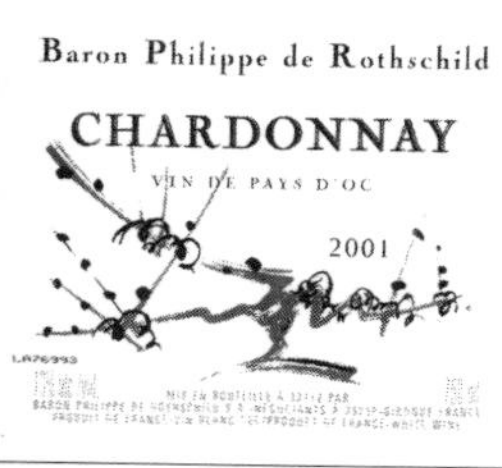

TRIMBACH 2000 PINOT BLANC, Alsace, France [#89292 $12.10] has a lively spirit and a warm heart – the wine equivalent of your best buddy. Pinot Blanc is often described as Chardonnay's more modest cousin.

DOM. PERRIN 2001 CÔTES DU LUBERON 'LA VIEILLE FERME', France [#298505 $9.95] has the generous flavours and freshness that inexpensive French whites lacked in the past. A dangerously delicious house wine – the height of simple satisfaction.

a walk on the wild side

one of wine's great sideshows – sauvignon blanc

In the mood for wine for seafood, Thai dishes, mildly spicy/hot foods or just to kick-start the taste buds.

The exuberant, fresh statement of Sauvignon is often likened to a spring breeze, but in some cases it's more like a winter gale. It's the jolt we desire when our mood is to feel more alive, to have a lift. The palate is certainly keener after a glass of Sauvignon.

Sauvignon Blanc is today's most exciting white wine category because it's so distinctive, and because the overall quality is very high. And the prices are reasonable. It is catching our attention for the same reasons that Asian food did – bright flavours and new sensations for the mouth. We may always return to Chardonnay for comfort and

luxury, but Sauvignon is the new choice for our adventurous times.

My approach to Sauvignon is to open it when the palate needs a jolt. There is no better refreshment on a hot day or a more uplifting drink to kick off dinner. Get a few bottles of my picks and see for yourself. I promise it will be an adventure. Any food that welcomes a 'squirt of lime' or a 'sprig of coriander' is a good partner for this wine. Cuisines in which the elements don't melt together, but bounce off each other are also natural partners for Sauvignon.

Service

Sauvignon needs to be really cold. A medium-sized glass is good, but for casual times a tumbler or juice glass will fit the off beat nature of the wine.

continued . . .

One sip of **VILLA MARIA 2001 SAUVIGNON BLANC 'PRIVATE BIN', New Zealand** [#409862 $13.95] and you'll see why New Zealand is considered to be the king of Sauvignon wines. It's a spa day in a bottle. Pure, herbal fragrances and vitality renew body and spirit – creating an immense appetite for food and life.

STONELEIGH 2002 SAUVIGNON BLANC, New Zealand [#293043 $13.05] is a pure, lip-smacking wine with a nice combination of exuberance and charm.

SANTA RITA 2002 SAUVIGNON BLANC, Chile [#275677 $11.35] is a real blast of zesty lime and other fruits. It's like a wild roller coaster ride – one of the great experiences in wine. A must try.

SEREGO ALIGHIERI 2001 BIANCO, Veneto, Italy [#409862 $12.95] a live wire that will show well in the company of seafood.

CAVE SPRING 2001 SAUVIGNON BLANC, Ontario [#529933 $12.95] is almost mild-mannered and would be a good first Sauvignon buy for the novice. Enjoy with fettucine alfredo.

For a fun, exotic take on Sauvignon try **MISSION HILL 2000 SAUVIGNON BLANC, Okanagan Valley, British Columbia** [#118893 $11.90]. Makes me want to dig out old Beach Boy records and have a party.

P.S. All of these wines would be ideal as aperitifs to kick off a dinner party.

chill out with a real nice white

the comfy side of everyday wine

In the mood for wines for comfort food, or just to sip.

OKAY. It's the moment you've all been waiting for. A few nice wines. A trip to Pleasant ville. Enjoy.

service

Served chilled in medium-sized glasses.

KONZELMANN'S 2000 PINOT BLANC, Ontario [#219279 $9.95] is one of our best locals when you're in the mood for something nice. Very fruity, very smooth and lip-smacking good.

SANTA MARGHERITA 2001 PINOT GRIGIO, Trentino, Italy [#106460 $13.85] is so nice that it has become the number one sellin imported white America. A good m of pleasantness an refreshment.

The best cheap date in this category is **MARQUES DE RISCAL Rueda, Spain** [#36822 $7.90]. Cuddles on a soft couch with a bowl of shrimp on the side.

[C]OLIO 2001 CHARDONNAY [C]HARROW ESTATES', [O]ntario [#432062 $8.95] is [q]uite laid back and easy to [liv]e with. Nice in a nice way.

Finally, there's **FETZER 2001 SUNDIAL CHARDONNAY, California** [#291674 $14.95]. Wine doesn't get any nicer.

P.S. Be warned – nice wine is low energy wine. Don't plan a party around this wine style.

the connoisseur's white

freshly starched shirt – dry riesling

<u>**In the mood for**</u> elegance. While Dry Riesling works well with almos all seafood or white meats, the main reason to select it is for its elegant an understated flavours. This is not for pizza or hockey night.

Riesling is confusing because it is made in many different styles. Earlier in the book I rec ommended a few live wire varieties for refreshment – here you'll find wines with a littl more flesh on them. Wines with the cool and elegant feeling of starched, white cotton

<u>service</u>

Serve well chilled in fine glassware.

CAVE SPRING 2000 RIESLING RESERVE, Ontario [#286377 $14.95] and **HENRY OF PELHAM 2001 RIESLING RESERVE, Ontario** [#283291 $12.65] have been two of Canada's best wines for almost a decade. Their cool, mineral flavours seem to vibrate in the glass. Wines to get you set up, to tease or to echo the fresh feeling in seafood. But they also have some body. If you pour dry Riesling before dinner and finish the bottle with seafood appetizers, your dinner party will be off to a great start. Your friends will think you are a wine wizard.

In the summer, give these wines a table in the sun with a white tablecloth and a vase of flowers. Think bright, Picasso colours and sharp edges.

CAVE SPRING
Reserve Réserve
RIESLING
VQA NIAGARA PENINSULA VQA
ESTATE BOTTLED
CAVE SPRING CELLARS, JORDAN, ONTARIO, CANADA
WHITE WINE/PRODUCT OF CANADA • VIN BLANC/PRODUIT DU CANADA
13.0% alc./vol. 750 mL

Q: Who developed Riesling?

A: The same people who make the purest lager and the most precision built cars.

medium red

Wines in the mid-range to celebrate the everyday.

FOR EVERYDAY MEALS

WINES THAT ARE ON THE FULLER SIDE OF MEDIUM.

FOOD PAIRING: mainly red meats – burgers, meatloaf, BBQ's, ribs, casseroles.

These are the wines that sit on the dinner table in the homes of the old wine countries, and on the tables in bistros, trattorias and tavernas. They're about sociability + aiding digestion. Some days they will seem heavenly, and other times just good company.

WATCHPOINT: Drink and enjoy all MEDIUM wines without too much fuss. Refrigerated open bottles will keep well for 3 to 4 days.

comfort reds

make people feel good

In the mood for red wine to partner with comfort food. Meatloaf, ribs or steak. Something with a lot of nourishment.

Some wines have their features built in to the very first sip, but the following unfold their goods over the evening. Warmth and nourishment are placed in the bottom half of the bottle.

service

Barely chill and serve in large glasses.

CANTINA TOLLO 1998 MONTEPULCIANO D'ABRUZZO 'COLLE SECCO', Italy [#195826 $8.15] may seem serious at first but it's not long before it reveals its warm heart. Amazing depth of character for the price. Like good meatloaf, it will never let you down.

PASQUA 1999 PRIMITIVO 'TERRE DEL SOLE', Italy [#561928 $8.95] has delicious ripe flavours and vitality. Yummy wine with a sense of good cheer. And good value.

UMANI RONCHI 1999 ROSSO CONERO 'SERRANO', Italy [#521096 $9.95] is a beefier, richer edition of its neighbour, Montepulciano D'Abruzzo. Characterful, nourishing wine with great drinkability.

a little rustic

wines with an edge

In the mood for wines with bite – putting niceness on hold for one night. Because an edge helps to stimulate the appetite and aids in the digestion of large meals.

All wines were rustic at one time. It used to be that smoothness was neither possible nor desirable. Few wines are rustic today because it is not a popular feature. Too bad, because it's one of those 'faults' that's really a blessing.

service

Barely chill and serve in medium-sized glasses.

RTANT DE FRANCE 2000 SYRAH, VDP D'OC, ance [#241510 $8.95] is everyday Syrah

with the gutsy, rustic character of French café wine. Not for the ns of smooth. It starts out slowly, unfolding as u drink. Equally good with white or red meat.

For Merlot with an appetizing bite, check out **PELEE ISLAND 2000 MERLOT, Ontario** [#612622 $11.95]. Wine for a table laden with a hearty dish of lamb or beef.

would be hard to find a better example of stic Italian red wine than **CITRA 2001 ONTEPULCIANO D'ABBRUZZO, Italy** [#446633

$6.65]. Great with hearty pasta, spicy sausages or even a steak. Italian house wine.

BACH 1999 VINA EXTRISIMA, Catalonia, Spain [#64014 $9.90] has super, ripe flavours but the main experience is tangy dryness. Very invigor-

ating. Though it is not instantly likeable, it invites you to hang in. Really gets the taste buds going. Very char-acterful for the price. Suggests a roasted bird or a braised dish.

HENRY OF PELHAM 2001 BACO NOIR, Ontario [#270926 $11.95] will appeal to those who enjoy fruity reds with an exuberant vitality. Beaujolais meets Barbera. It's Ontario's most distinctive red. A little quirky. A light chill brings out the magic. With a burger it tastes like a million bucks.

chillin' out

the height of simple satisfaction

In the mood for red wine that's instantly satisfying. Wine that friendly, fun and an easy fit. Wine for anything. Wine for spicy food.

service

Barely chill and serve in medium-sized glasses.

TORRES 2000 SANGRE DE TORO, Catalonia, Spain [#6585 $10.45] is a cheerful red that's been the best thing out of Spain for the last decade. It has a bright, lively good-for-the-soul quality that we associate with the Mediterranean life. I've yet to find a food or event that it did not complement. A light chill makes it even more satisfying.

MOMMESSIN 2001 CÔTES DU RHONE 'LES EPICES', France [#14829 $10.95] fills the mouth with ripe fruitiness and a feeling of warmth and nourishment. Wine to cuddle up to – a charmer. Although it's sort of rich, there is no heaviness or seriousness. The duvet of rich reds perhaps. The perfect fall or winter red.

FORTANT DE FRANCE 2001 MERLOT, VDP D'OC, France [#293969 $8.95] has a delicious, spicy quality that adds interest to Merlot's plummy, fruit flavours. There's fullness and generosity, but also some play and charm. A lot of treats for the price. Try with a big, juicy burger, or a spiced-up lamb or chicken dish. Buy for parties for sure.

H. DE BARCELO 2000 PENASCAL CASTILLA Y LEON, Spain [#343434 $8.95] is not from Rioja but it's identical in style – mellow/sweet with strawberry, spice and tobacco flavours. Cuddly, charming and nourishing. Sexy too. Quite the show for the price. Wine for beef, burgers, and sausages. The spicier the better. Chill lightly

deep feelings

reds for mellow moods

In the mood for a fireside red.

What a treat it is to be able to buy red wines with deep, mature flavours for only te or twelve bucks. Plan the night, pick up a few bottles and relax. Mellow reds are be with simple grilled or roasted meats and vegetables.

service

Serve in very large glasses at room temperature.

AGRICOLE VALLONE 1998 SALICE SALENTINO 'VERETO', Italy [#471730 $10.10] feels generous and rich in a genuine, down-to-earth way.

VERETO
AGRICOLE VALLONE
ITALIA
SALICE SALENTINO
denominazione di origine controllata
ROSSO
RED WINE - VIN ROUGE
1998
Estate Bottled by
Mis en bouteille à la propriété par
AGRICOLE VALLONE
LECCE - ITALY
nella propria cantina di Copertino
PRODUCT OF ITALY - PRODUIT D'ITALIE

The charm, warmth and soulful character of an old country inn – faded elegance, as it is often called. Every time I have this wine I wonder why I don't buy it more often. Don't let that happen to you.

SOGRAPE 1999 DAO 'DUQUE DE VISEU', Portugal #546309 $12.65] is a nourishing, comfort wine that also has a rustic country feeling. Quite mellow, smokey . . . and maybe sexy. Very good stuff.

VINHOS V SOGRAPE

DUQUE DE VISEU

DÃO

Denominação de Origem Controlada

RED WINE - VIN ROUGE

1999

BULLETIN PLACE 1999 MERLOT, Australia [#598805 $11.60] is a delicious, silky wine that flirts between the luxurious and the everyday. Seductive without being rich or heavy. An invitation to enjoy often.

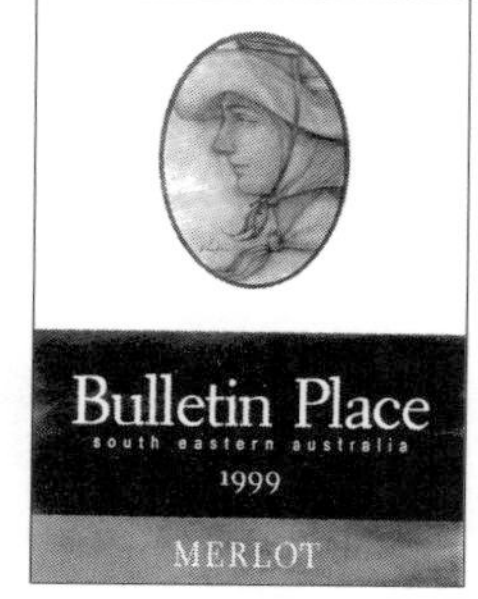

best for burgers

we're working on it

In the mood for wine to wash down your best BBQ'd burger.

There are probably as many ideas on what constitutes a good burger as there are peop who enjoy them. The best wine choice is sure to be subjective too. Here's mine. Becaus burgers offer instant gratification, I select a wine that tastes good from the first sip. Th wine must also have an appetizing bite because I want the last mouthful to taste as goo as the first. New World, fruity wines are usually best, especially if you like to load up c burger fixings. As ever, it's a mood thing. But not a matter of life and death.

service

Serve in tumblers or medium-sized glasses. Lightly chill.

ROSEMOUNT 2001 SHIRAZ/CABERNET, Australia [#214270 $13.45] must surely have been created by the burger gods. Or by someone who's

spent many an evening tuning in to the flavours and feelings created by a BBQ'd burger. It makes the experience bigger and richer – and does it with a sense of play. A great food and wine match for sure.

TALUS 1999 SHIRAZ, California [#605501 $11.95] is cheerful, lively, and quite charming. Born to be at every party. Lightly chill. It might be the most seductive red in the store.

Another fun style wine choice is **CONO SUR 2001 PINOT NOIR, Chile** [#341602 $9.95]. Cheerful, high-spirited, slightly smokey stuff to chill and gulp before, during and after your burger. It wants to party.

COLIO HARROW ESTATE 2000 CABERNET FRANC, Ontario [#297184 $9.95] has a nice, friendly, everyday quality that falls somewhere between Beaujolais and Shiraz. Its spicy, cheer-

ful nature is a perfect fit for hamburger night. Or poker night. A good party choice too. Chill lightly.

Rounding out our international line is **SOGRAPE 2000 DOURO 'VILLA REGIA', Portugal** [#464388 $7.70]. It has delicious fruitiness and a friendly twinkle. And a friendly price.

P.S. Just about any wine in this MEDIUM RED section would be a good partner for a burger.

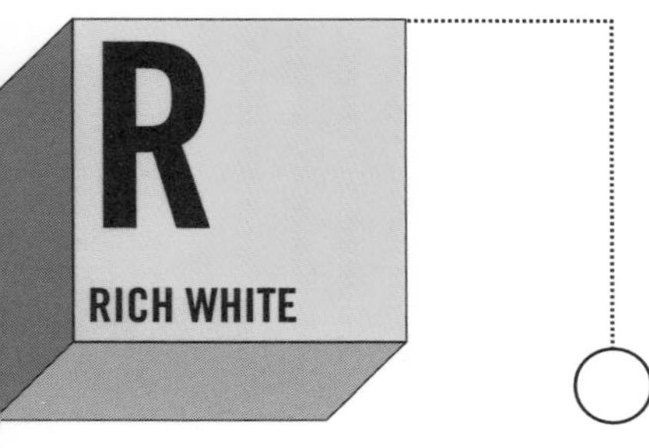

rich white

'or mellow moods + the comfort of substantial meals.

THE HEAVYWEIGHTS

HE RICH FEELING. EXCESS. SUBSTANTIAL WINES FOR SUBSTANTIAL MEALS.
R JUST TO SIP.

OOD PAIRING: seafood, rich chicken dishes, BBQ's or spicy dishes that suggest white wine.

low paced and expansive. Don't have RICH wines until you are ready for flat out relaxation.

ATCHPOINT: Good glassware will echo the sense of luxury and glamour in these wines.
efrigerated open bottles will keep well for 3 to 4 days.

local riches

special occasion Chardonnays

In the mood for a slow-paced dinner with a rich chicken or seafoo dish. A mellow mood.

Chardonnay's lovely, exotic flavours and toasty richness are an exciting show when the reveal themselves gradually. The following two wines are beautiful examples of slo unfolding. Plan a dinner. Find a recipe for herbed chicken or grilled salmon and polis up some nice glassware.

service

Serve cold – but not icy cold – in fine stemware.

There is a confidence and lushness to **CAVE SPRING 2000 CHARDONNAY 'ESTATE', Ontario** [#471391 $14.95] that makes you feel that you are seated in a fancy restaurant enjoying good company and good food. A delicious, stylish, well-made wine that keeps Cave Spring at the top end of local Chardonnays.

HENRY OF PELHAM 2000 CHARDONNAY 'BARREL FERMENTED', Ontario [#268342 $22.95] is a lovely mix of richness, vibrant flavours, and lemon freshness. It feels very alive and pure for such a big wine. The classy statement that local wines are capable of, but which few winemakers achieve [or desire].

P.S. Many local, rich Chardonnays are produced in limited quantities and sold directly at the winery. For some of the best, visit **CHATEAU DES CHARMES, HILLEBRAND, INNISKILLIN, JACKSON-TRIGGS, MALIVOIRE, PELLER ESTATES, SOUTHBROOK, LENKO, THIRTEENTH STREET,** and **CREEKSIDE.**

rich whites for under $10

luxury wine at workingman's prices

In the mood for exotic wine to partner with a summer BBQ or dinn party. Or just to sip.

Rich wines used to be rare and expensive but not anymore. Any Dick or Jane can no afford a date with these exotic delights. At the dinner table or on the couch. Some these wines are quite the sensual, sexy experience. Fortunately, they don't mention thi on the label so there is no need to be embarrassed at the checkout.

service

Serve cold – not too cold – in fairly large stemware. Pretend you spent a bundle.

FORTANT DE FRANCE 2001 CHARDONNAY VDP D'OC, France [#256560 $8.45] is an upstart French winery that's making stunning budget-priced wines. The 2001 Chardonnay has Rolls Royce smoothness and lushness.

SINNYA VALLEY 2001 CHARDONNAY, South Africa [#566067 $9.95] offers a lovely cuddle along with a lively personality. Charm and drinkability are the features here.

SANTA RITA 2001 CHARDONNAY '120', Chile [#315184 $8.75] has huge tropical flavours and a down 'n dirty personality. Raunchy, masculine, white wine. BBQ wine for sure.

Another South African, **KWV 2002 CHARDONNAY, South Africa** [#304360 $8.95] is quite the creamy mouthful. Imagine booking into a budget motel and finding down-filled pillows. Needs charred flavours in the food to balance the plushness. Or you could just sip and swoon.

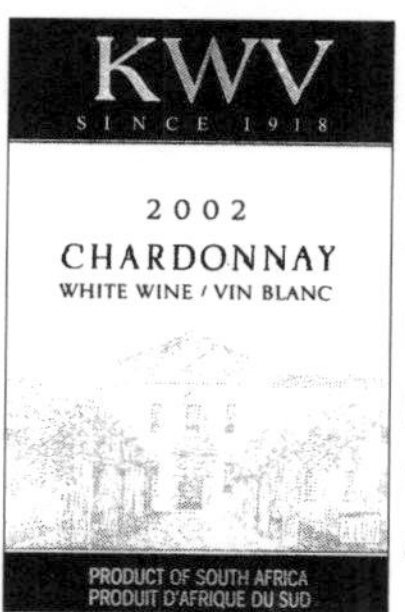

rich 'n tangy

with a bite

In the mood for BBQ white wines. Rich whites that have a fondn for foods with a charred or roasted flavour. A good partner for turkey too.

A tangy bite is important in rich wine. It makes the wine more appetizing and preven the richness from tiring our senses. It also provides an edge in the same way th grilling or BBQ'ing adds a bitter edge to foods.

service

Serve cold – but not too cold – in fairly fancy stemware.

The savoury/tangy character of **KENDALL-JACKSON 2000 SEMILLON/CHARDONNAY 'COLLAGE', California** [#567636 $15.40] cries out for something from the BBQ. It is the nature of the Semillon to lead the drinker to food. While it lacks the glamour of Chardonnay, it makes up for this in food friendliness.

WOLF BLASS CHARDONNAY, South Australia [#226860 $14.95] used to have crowd-pleasing niceness but the current 2001 vintage is much drier. A lemony tang provides a pleasant contrast to the tropical flavours. Great white wine for seafood. Or a simple roast chicken.

lovely but not loud

hidden richness

In the mood for dinner party wine that won't try to upstage yo
food or friends.

Here are a couple of wines that offer the comforts and luxury of a big car – without th
fuss. Talented but not showy.

service

Serve cold – but not too cold – in fairly fancy stemware.

If there were to be a Cinderella wine at the LCBO it would surely be **LEON BEYER 2000 TOKAY-PINOT GRIS, Alsace, France** [#165241 $14.95]. This Alsace white has the richness of Chardonnay but it feels fresher and more elegant. Dinner party rather than BBQ. A slight spiciness invites similar notes in food. Well-seasoned grilled salmon or chicken would be dandy.

SIMONSIG 2000 CHARDONNAY, South Africa [#345389 $12.45] is another talented but modest wine. Sleek rather than showy. The first glass is refreshing with a wonderful tease of flavours and richness. Smart dinner party wine. Your friends will think it's French and expensive.

Chile's amazing wine show

budget priced luxury

In the mood for big white wine experiences for dinner partie BBQ's or just to sip.

Chile doesn't yet have a reputation for superior wines, so many of its deluxe wine effor are underpriced. The following pair may well be the greatest wine bargains to be ha from anywhere in the world today. Luxury wines at everyday prices. Get 'em while you ca

P.S. These wines will welcome bold-flavoured or even spicy/hot foods. Another idea is forget mealtimes – sip on a glass each evening for a nightcap.

service

This is one time when I'd recommend using a large glass for a white wine – you don't want to miss any these great flavours. While your first glass would be good cold, subsequent ones should be less so in order get the full show of flavour.

MIGUEL TORRES 2001 GEWURZTRAMINER, Chile [#605584 $11.75] confused me at first and then I smartened up and let it climb all over me. What flavour and sensations it delivers. But forget expectations about Gewurztraminer – this is more akin to a big, bold, brazen Aussie Chardonnay. A full-bodied, well-tanned surfer for sure. Amazingly fresh, tangy and invigorating for such a rich wine. Could be the world's best drink partner for chicken or turkey. You gotta try it.

ANTA RITA 2000 CHARDONNAY RESERVA, Chile #348359 $11.95] has consistently been one of .e best values in rich whites since I started ublishing this annual handbook. It's like taying at the Ritz for student prices. A mix of opical flavours, creamy richness and a vitality at's often missing in rich wines.

ich red

or mellow moods + the comfort of substantial meals.

HE HEAVYWEIGHTS

IE RICH FEELING. EXCESS. SUBSTANTIAL WINES FOR SUBSTANTIAL MEALS. OR JUST TO SIP.

OOD PAIRING: big steak, lamb rack, roasts or rich, braised meats.

ow paced and expansive. Don't have RICH wines until you are ready for flat out relaxation.

ATCHPOINT: Good glassware will echo the sense of luxury and glamour in these wines.
efrigerated open bottles will keep well for 3 to 4 days.

shir-az-nice

the crowd-pleaser

In the mood for wine that's as nourishing and seductive as choc late. A big red for a big steak or burger.

Aussie Shiraz is the red equivalent of Chardonnay. A rich, glamour wine. It's a big h because it fulfills our desire for instant gratification with its softness, smoothness a sweet/chocolate flavours. As someone once said, "Shiraz tastes like Christmas day."

The experience of Shiraz can be similar to the in-your-face character of popular ente tainment today. Little is left to the imagination, there is no buildup, there is no myste – you get it all right away. And you get lots.

I've selected wines that I think are the most food friendly – and which won't exhau your senses. At least for the first hour.

service

Serve in huge goblets at room temperature.

HARDY'S 2000 'NOTTAGE HILL' SHIRAZ, Australia [#373964 $12.45] is a playful, drink anytime, edition of Shiraz. Bright, spirited, with yummy, spicy/sweet flavours. So much fun. Especially good for parties. Chill lightly.

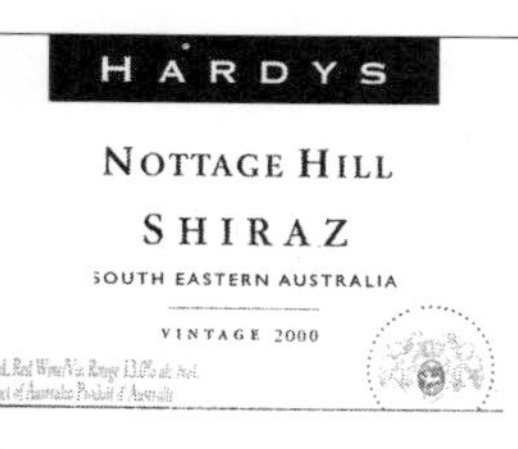

FIDDLERS CREEK 2000 SHIRAZ/CABERNET, Australia [#560498 $13.25] is a big, hearty wine. Manly, solid stuff for a big meal. Should get better and better over the next few years.

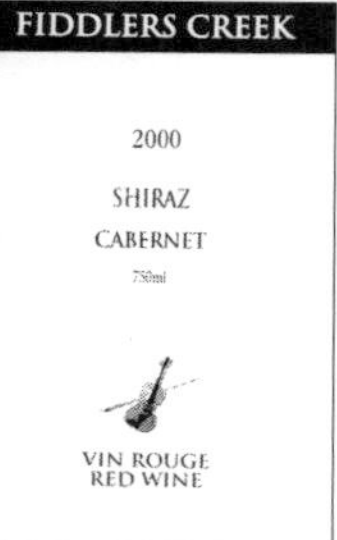

WYNDHAM ESTATE 2000 'BIN 555' SHIRAZ, Australia [#189415 $14.60] is port-like. Dark, with huge flavours, especially chocolate. Very sweet. A winter warmer. Sure to be popular.

HOUGHTON 1999 SHIRAZ, Western Australia [#338673 $16.00] is a great mouthful of spicy, exotic flavour. Very rich but also very exuberant. Sip slowly.

P.S. **WOLF BLASS** and **ROSEMOUNT** are the big sellers in this category but their wines are tight and raw – too young to drink. The demand for Shiraz is forcing producers to send wine to market before it's ready to be drunk.

the ripassos

sexy Italians

In the mood for rich wine that won't fill you up. Wine with old fashioned charm.

The Valpolicella region in the north of Italy is best known for inexpensive, light reds to drink with pizza, and for a rich, hedonistic wine called Amarone. An in-between style of red, called Ripasso, is also produced and it's awfully good. And reasonably priced.

Ripassos are drier and more appetizing than most rich reds. They are great partners for a broad range of foods, from Italian tomato-sauced foods, to fowl and even steak.

service

Serve in big glasses at slightly less than room temperature.

SEREGO ALIGHIERI 2000 VALPOLICELLA CLASSICO, Italy [#447326 $14.50] starts out appetizing and refreshing. Nourishing richness and belly-warming, woodsy/berry flavours settle in later. So invigorating, so soulful, so charming. So good on a winter's night.

PASQUA 1999 'SAGRAMOSO' RIPASSO VALPOLICELLA, Italy [#602342 $14.95] goes deep in the flavour and character departments.

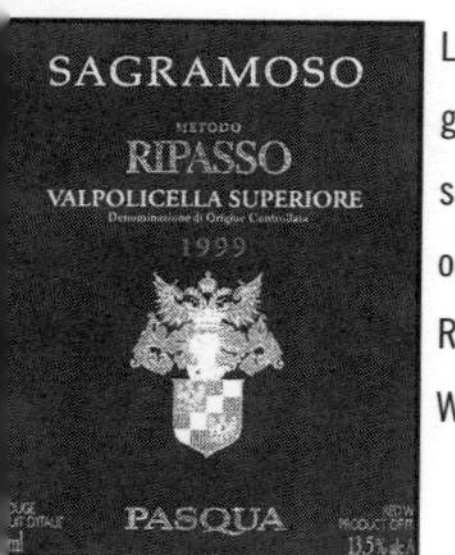

Lots of Italian gusto and passion. The manly one of the Ripasso group. Wine for beef.

CESARI 1999 'MARA' RIPASSO VALPOLICELLA, Italy [#506519 $13.90] is the smooth guy and big charmer of the Ripasso brigade. Mellow richness borders on Californian and Aussie styling but it keeps its Italian vitality. May be the yummiest red wine on the planet. A fireside drink for sure.

merry merlot

the champion of richness

In the mood for a rich red.

When it comes to selecting the world's favourite red, it's a toss up between Merlot an Shiraz. Merlot fans will argue that it's got a greater range of styles and uses and tha it's more elegant. It can also be voluptuous, as you'll discover when you try the wine opposite.

service

Serve in large glasses at room temperature.

ODEGAS LA RURAL 2001 MERLOT TRUMPETER', Argentina [#467985 $13.30] s certainly out to please. It provides the smooth, glowing' experience that we associate with a omantic, candlelit steak dinner. Check it out.

OBERT SKALLI 2000 MERLOT VDP D'OC, rance [#571042 $12.95] is full of warmth and chness. Earthy too. It's the Full Monty of lerlots. Big time nourishment at a most reasonble price. Plan the big night. Porterhouse peraps. Skalli is the Fortant de France guy that we et in the Medium section. High quality at veryday prices is Skalli's forte. I'll drink to that.

HARDYS 1999 CABERNET/SHIRAZ/MERLOT, Australia [#565119 $15.15] is a 'best of all worlds' wine, offering a voluptuous feeling and a solid nature – great for steak. Warmhearted and capable of being fancy or 'just-for-fun'.

P.S. Merlot wines have shown up in all three red sections of this book. A confusing wine, eh!

big seducers

Hollywood style

In the mood for sensual reds.

While some rich reds exude power, others appeal in a more teasing, exotic way. Pin Noir is known as the wine of lovers because of its seductive, feminine nature. When yo find a good one it's an instant love affair. Winemakers can also craft other grape va ieties with hedonistic appeal. We need all the love we can get.

service

Serve lightly chilled in big glasses.

FETZER 2000 PINOT NOIR 'VALLEY OAKS', California [#425447 $15.95] is the kind of wine that gets you to spend above your budget. Seductive wine to make you lose control. Very sweet, very silky and very sexy. Flavours of middle eastern spices. Great with any well-seasoned dishes. And a romantic mood.

MISSION HILL 2000 CABERNET/MERLOT, British Columbia [#257816 $13.45] is silky and loaded with spicy/sweet flavours. Very seductive, very Californian. A bit over-the-top maybe, but who cares?

R.H. PHILLIPS 2000 SYRAH, DUNNIGAN HILLS, California [#576272 $16.55] is the Californian edition of Chateauneuf-Du-Pape – big, rich and spicy. Instant seduction. Lush wine for a winter's evening.

CHAPOUTIER 1999 CÔTES DU RHÔNE-VILLAGES, RASTEAU, France [#32159 $14.95] is the Rhône's contribution to the world of seductive, sexy red wine. Beautifully scented, with delicate, teasing sweet berry/herbal flavours. Graceful, lush – but spirited too. Better with a bird than with beef.

Gourgazaud + Guigal

a couple of french names

In the mood for rich reds.

Minervois is in the French Languedoc region, which has become France's new win world. The past decade has seen an amazing make-over and now Languedoc's vineyar size is twice that of Australia's – and just as modern. And every bit as sunny, a Languedoc is located in the extreme southwest. The focus is mainly on good everyda wine, and lots of it. While the wines have hot climate ripeness, they tend to be less over the-top than Aussie wine.

service

Serve in large glasses at room temperature.

CH. DE GOURGAZAUD, MINERVOIS, France [#22384 $10.05] has been around for years but has never been as good as this 2001 vintage. Deep, dark fruit and spicy flavours create the warm glow of a fireside. Lots of richness for the price. When did you last buy a bottle of Chateau something for only ten dollars?

France's Rhone region has a long established tradition for good value reds and Mr. Guigal's wine has been recommended in every issue of this book. **GUIGAL 1999 CÔTES DU RHÔNE, France** [#25972 $15.70] is a substantial, dark-coloured wine. Guigal always crafts for richness and full flavours so expect big-hug warmth. The sweet, peppery flavours suggest beef or lamb, but a good homemade burger would not be out of line. Look for more flavour and lushness to unfold in a year or two.

cathedrals of red wine

the high and mighty – power wine

In the mood for a red that will make you feel like an emperor.

One sip of these wines and you'll see why Cabernet is the favourite wine of power seekers. It exudes power. It has huge ego.

Wines this rich and powerful need long evenings at the dinner table. Drink enough and you may still be there in the morning.

service

Serve in large glasses at room temperature.

SANTA RITA 2000 CABERNET SAUVIGNON RESERVE, Chile [#253872 $11.80] is the bargain in the power wine league. Has the big flavour thing but there's also an earthy, firm side. More sturdy than sexy.

ERRAZURIZ 1999 CABERNET SAUVIGNON RESERVA 'DON MAXIMIANO', Chile [#335174 $17.95] is the daddy in this group because it is the richest. And it's starting to mellow. Suggests porterhouse steak and a powerfully perfumed cigar. It would be a crime not to use a large glass.

PELEE ISLAND 2000 CABERNET/MERLOT, Ontario [#4353211 $14.95] is quite robust. Would welcome the company of a platter of ribs and a few cattle ranchers.

Please be seated for **WYNN'S 1999 COONAWARRA CABERNET SAUVIGNON, Australia** [#502039 $18.95] because it is an overwhelming experience. It's hard to imagine how they got so much flavour and richness into the bottle. I dare you to tackle this on a weeknight.

fringe wines

FOR SIPPING + CELEBRATING

EXTRA EASY

EXTRA SWEET

EXTRA STRONG

THE MISCELLANEOUS

sparkling wines $10 - $14

getting the right bubbles

In the mood for fun!

I've recommended a few sparkling wines in the FRESH section and they are repeated here so you don't forget to include them in your party shopping.

WITH A LITTLE FOOD

Sparkling wine with food is not well understood. The yeasty, fleshy flavour in Spanish sparklers is an ideal partner for tapas or other Mediterranean appetizers. The acid and fizz in the wine make a refreshing swipe through the oil and garlic. This style of sparkler is also good with savoury, pastry appetizers of the quiche or Greek variety, and with tempura or sushi. Again, the wine cuts the fat, butter or batter.

Both of these wines have been consistently good for as long as I can remember.

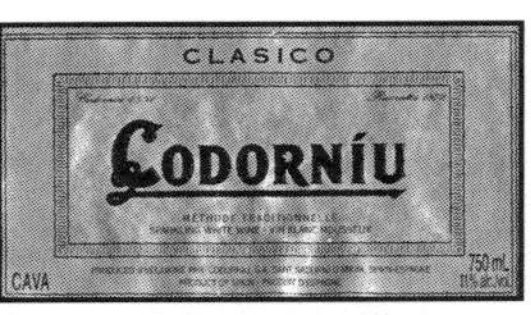

CODORNIU BRUT CLASSICO, Spain [#503490 $10.

SEGURA VIUDAS BRUT, Spain [#158493 $11.45]

OR REFRESHMENT
R TO GET THE PARTY STARTED

ith so many good, inexpensive sparkling ines around it's a pity that more people don't tart their events with a glass of fizz. I asked arry Mawby [maker of sparkling wine in orthern Michigan] why people are reluctant to njoy reasonably priced sparkling wines on a aily basis. "People are afraid that the occa- ion is not worthy of the wine."

ROSECCO DI VALDOBBIADENE 2001 BRUT, aly [#340570 $11.60]

EAKIN ESTATE BRUT, Australia
#876264 $11.95]

ACOB'S CREEK BRUT CUVEÉ HARDONNAY/PINOT NOIR, Australia
#562991 $13.25]

champagne $40 - $50

wine of the imagination

In the mood for celebration!

a] Half of the cost of a bottle of Champagne is not for the drink but for the aura. Billions of dollars have been, and will always be, spent to create magic around the drinking of Champagne. Like religion, the more you believe, the more you get out of it. If you're not a believer, you should not waste your money on Champagne. The experience is like being at a fancy restaurant where you're paying as much for the magic in the room as for the food on the plate.

b] Champagne is a sour [vibrant nervosity, in wine lingo], mildly flavoured drink with none of the instant 'wow' of a good Icewine, Port, Chardonnay or rich red. It's more feel than flavour. More about promise than show. Champagne, however, is associated with celebration and ritual and one may want to uphold the tr dition even if one gets no great pleasure from the drin

c] Many deluxe and vintage-dated Champagnes a offered by the Board and you may wonder if a hu dred dollars will buy a bigger thrill than spending mere forty or fifty. These Champagnes can be twic the experience, but only for those who are alrea familiar with Champagne.

d] You will get more out of Champagne if you drir it at quiet times when there are not too many di tractions. The subtlety of the drink is lost if there too much going on.

ᵻEST APERITIF CHAMPAGNE

ɦe following three Champagnes have the teas-
ıg, uplifting quality that's great before dinner.

OL ROGER BRUT, France
ᵻ51953 $44.95]

ICOLAS FEUILLATE BRUT, France
ᵻ537605 $39.85]

IPER-HEIDSIECK BRUT, France
ᵻ361626 $42.95]

BEST SIPPING CHAMPAGNE

CHARLES HEIDSIECK BRUT N/V, France
[#31286 $47.95]

CHARLES HEIDSIECK is the Buick of Champagnes – soft and luxurious, a smooth ride and good enough to get noticed. Makes a lovely, pleasing statement. Great anytime.

THE CHAMPAGNE WORD

In case you don't know, the word Champagne is exclusive to the wines of that region in France. All other bubbly wines must simply be called 'sparkling'. You will get more respect from LCBO and restaurant staff when you display your understanding of this point.

not-so-dry wines

party, patio or garden wines

<u>In the mood for</u> easy-sipping wines.

Summer is the best season to enjoy this 'aromatic' category of wines because of the garden-like flavours and lighthearted feeling, and because the low alcohol allows fo serious gulping. They're especially good on any deck or dock, and with Sunday brunch. Not so-dry wines offer a change of pace, which is what seasons are all about. Serve all thes wines quite cold because that will emphasize their zest and balance the fruity sweetnes

Good cheer is the message in **CAVE SPRING 2001 OFF-DRY RIESLING, Ontario** [#234583 $11.25]. Refreshing as well as tasty.

BALACH 99 RIVERSIDE RIESLING, Germany

[#499814 $9.95] is a light, fruity sipper. Peachy.

PELEE ISLAND 2001 GEWURZTRAMINER, Ontario [#135970 $10.45] always delights with its zany flavour and gentle, easy drinkability. Great with eggs.

ODEGA LURTON 2001 PINOT GRIS, Argentina

[#556746 $8.95] has a zesty, fresh fruit quality that would go over well in the summertime. A crowd-pleaser for sure.

A medium-dry sparkler is a good idea for parties because not everyone likes bone-dry wines. **MARTINI & ROSSI'S DEMI-SEC, Italy** [#415372 $10.80] is clean and refreshing with not a trace of candy. Try a bottle for a pre-lunch or brunch pick-me-up.

sweet

little bottles

In the mood for something sweet.

These wines taste equally good in the winter or on hot, sultry summer evenings. Unfortunately, the selection has dwindled and many of the favourites from previous years are no longer around. The following is a rundown of the best available. Those living in major centres should visit a Vintages store or boutique for a better selection. I like to drink these wines cold because it tempers the sweetness. Opened bottles will keep well for a week stored in the fridge.

. . . very berry

SOUTHBROOK FARMS FRAMBOISE, Ontario [#341024 375ml/$14.45] is a liqueur-like wine made from raspberries. Try this one with a chocolate dessert.

. . . charmer

QUADY 'ESSENSIA' 1999 ORANGE MUSCAT, California [#299552 375ml/$14.60] is a real charmer from the Quady winery, which specializes in sweet drinks. Great with any 'caramel' dessert or just to sip. Chill.

. . *peachy*

OLLO ESTATES 2000 LATE HARVEST VIDAL, ntario [#470369 375ml/$9.95] is a great alue. Wonderful honey and peach flavours are alanced with a nutty tang. Enjoy with biscotti r an almond cake.

. . *luscious*

AVE SPRING 2000 SELECT LATE HARVEST IESLING 'INDIAN SUMMER', Ontario [#415901 375/$21.95] is a wonderful mix of tropical flavours and freshness. It's an uplifting feeling – really fills the mouth – but there is not a trace of sweetness in the aftertaste. Enjoy with cake or just on its own.

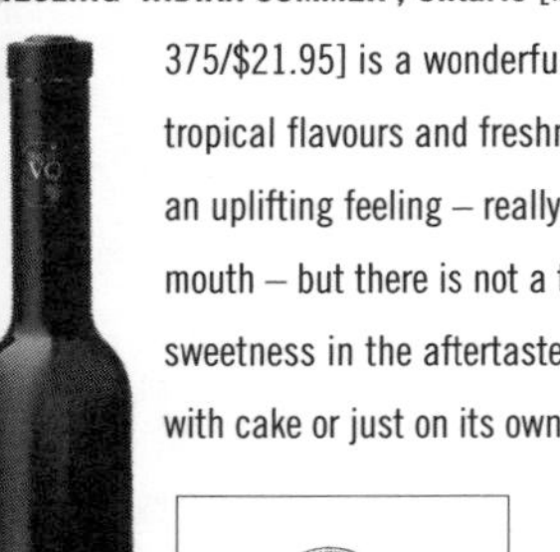

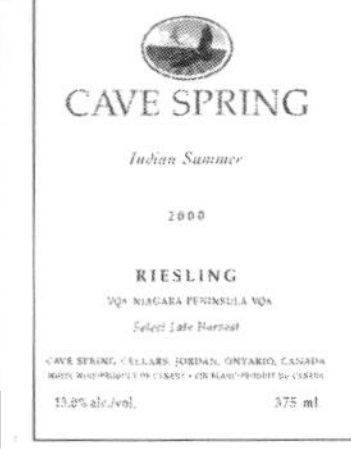

. . . *zesty*

While the initial sensation of **HENRY OF PELHAM 2000 SPECIAL SELECT LATE HARVEST VIDAL, Ontario** [#395228 375ml/$18.95] has luscious, sweet, peachy flavours, this wine also has a light and zesty character. It's as refreshing as it is sweet. The ideal little sip for after a summer lunch in the garden, or late evening on the porch, or 'whenever'.

a glass of port

strong, sweet stuff

In the mood for a heartwarming drink.

Buying Port is confusing because the $15 stuff looks exactly the same as the $75 stuf
The simplest explanation I can give is that the high-priced bottles are the equivalent c
aged single malts, and the others are bar scotch. The everyday varieties that I'm rec
ommending here should keep most people happy because the quality is very hig
Generally speaking, Ports with the wine Vintage anywhere on the label tend to be bol
dark and fiery. These are traditionally drunk at the end of a meal when you're in nee
of a strong drink. Tawny-style Ports are paler in colour and have a gracious, mello
character. The female side of Port. A cozy chair by the fireside is the venue for thes
Ports are usually served at room temperature but the Tawny style can be chilled. Ope
bottles will keep for several days – if you hide them.

rink a glass of **DELAFORCE RICH TAWNY, ortugal** [#154807 $14.20] and you'll find full uitiness and mellow charm. A bargain for veryday drinking.

RAHAM'S 10-YEAR-OLD-TAWNY, Portugal #206508 $27.95] is an exciting mix of fire nd silky texture. A great Tawny Port experience r the price.

AYLOR FLADGATE 1997 LATE BOTTLE VINTAGE, ortugal [#46946 $17.75] is serious. The abernet of Ports – dark, manly stuff to inspire reams of fame and fortune. Drink after dinner.

a glass of sherry

dry is best

In the mood for a strong wine.

Cheap Sherry is seldom good, but the real stuff, such as tangy dry FINO, nutty d AMONTILLADO, or rich DRY OLOROSO are fabulous drinks that are underpriced when yo consider the time and effort that goes into making them. With a few exceptions, all goo Spanish Sherry is dry, and hard to find. Your local LCBO will carry mainly the commer cial sweet brands but Vintages usually has a few of the styles I've mentiontioned. DR OLOROSO or AMONTILLADO have some of the most concentrated and exciting flavour to be found in any wine. Worth seeking out.

The lightest, palest, driest Sherry of all is called FINO and it is available. See opposit

'oducer Gonzalez Byass has dumped the tradi- ɔnal black garb and re-outfitted its TIO PEPE NO in a fresh, green package. Same bone-dry, isp, refreshing drink but it's amazing how uch more appeal it has now. Fino is a high cohol [about 15%] dry wine so it packs a ınch. A tang. It's a great hot weather aperitif partner for shrimps off the BBQ. A little Fino es a long way so it's quite the bargain. A frigerated open bottle keeps well for at least week.

ɔNZALEZ BYASS FINO 'TIO PEPE', Spain
242669 $14.95]

Wine pleasure has as much to do with what's in your head as what's in your glass."

wine stuff

ou need to know

hat's happening

hanges

etting started in wine

ervice

he good host

ine talk

ad thoughts

illy's 10 commandments

what's happening in wine

Wine in the $12 – $18 range

is providing us with previously unheard of quality/value bottles. It is being produced b both big and small wineries. The average person need not look further for their wine thrill

It gets better and better.

There is more good wine produced than we can drink. And some of it comes from place that don't charge a lot. Meanwhile, traditional, pricey wine regions are still trying every tric in the book to make us buy their wines – or to make us feel inferior if we don't.

The quality gap between the top and the bottom is much narrower.

There are few bad wines anymore – but there are lots of boring ones.

Wine has become 'product', made to meet a price point and a market taste.

While the quality may be decent, there is an uninspired 'sameness' that will lead to bo dom if you drink these wines too often. Australia is leading this enterprise. A lot of Australia and Californian wines under $12 are already tasting like pop.

Italy, Spain, Portugal and the south of France are the places producing the most interesting, and best value daily wines.

Local wine will continue finding its way into people's hearts and shopping baskets, as th quality of the everyday wines gets better and better. The sunshine spots, California and Australia, will lose fans by overcharging for not-so-great-wine. Chile and South Africa will be the best sources for value in rich wines, as long as you know what to buy.

go driven wine is on the increase.

Many of the world's wineries, no matter how average their quality, want to play with the superstars and are producing 'deluxe' wine for which they overcharge. While the wine is richer and more highly pefumed than the regular wine of the house, it often tastes unreal. You can tell it's been pushed beyond its capacity – creative overkill!

he wine industry continues to alienate otential customers.

with its elitist, snobby image and practices. Two-hundred-dollar-a-plate gala dinnners may impress a few, but they're a turn-off for the average person. I think that the public wants confirmation from winemakers [and the wine business] that the category of everyday-priced wine is worthwhile and every bit as special as the snobby stuff.

ew studies show that wine drinkers are healthier and ealthier.

A daily glass of red wine has been shown to help stave off heart disease and even cancer, but a Danish study said the grapes salutary effects may be due to imbibers' sense of well-being. "Our results suggest that wine drinking is associated with optimal social, intellectual and personality functioning,"states study author, Erik Mortensen, of the Danish Epidemiology Science Centre in Copenhagen.

wine has changed

in taste

Sometime in the past decade, modern-style wines took over. Wines perfumed with th vanilla and buttered toast flavour of oak have became the norm. Wine is now mor glamorous, a bit sweeter, and a lot easier to like. It seems to be following the ente tainment business with its focus on bigness, glitz and spectacle. This is risky. Every da in everyone's life does not need to be all bright and colourful. Wines need to echo all o moods and situations. Have Italian wine at least once a week.

in selection

New frontiers are opening up all the time so there are always new bargains. Wine g better when France lost its monopoly. She ruled the business for too long, and almos ruined it. Ironically, the places that gave us better wine (Australia and California) a now doing exactly what France did – overcharging and producing dull wines. Meanwhil France has learned how to make good everyday wine and is now the good guy. Th growth of our local wines has been the greatest joy of all. It makes wine more real f people who have never travelled to Europe.

and in the guidelines

Are there guidelines that one can follow such as, small producers are better than larg ones? Or hot climates are better than cool ones? No. Sorry. In the old days there was a nice clear distinction between the good guys and the bad guys, but these days everyone has the potential to get it right – if they try. Wine has changed and the old guidelines and beliefs are no longer reliable. To illustrate this, let's take a look at some of the wines recommended in this book in relation to some of the 'old rules'.

Riesling is a semi-sweet German wine that's popular with novices. Wrong. Ontario produces Dry Rieslings that are on par with the best Sauvignon Blancs or Chardonnays.

Big companies produce only bland, commercial wines. Wrong. Check out the Hardys and Fetzer recommendations.

Co-op wine is old-fashioned rotgut. Wrong. Abruzzi's Cantina Tollo co-op makes wine as modern as Mondavi.

You would never find a good, refreshing white from a 'backward' wine country such as Hungary. Wrong. Experience the wonderful, fresh fragrances and zest in Dunavar Muscat.

Italy only produces light reds for pasta or pizza. Wrong. Cesari's 'Mara' or Pasqua's Ripasso would do justice to the hulkiest steak or chop.

To approach wine with a full heart and an empty head. Anything is possible. The only thing you can be sure of is that the 'old rules' are no longer useful.

getting started in wine

Look for a buddy

to share the experience and the costs. Not a wine geek, but someone whos opinions you value.

Try lots of different wines at first

using my WINE SPECTRUM chart as a guide to what to expect. Always taste least two wines so you have a contrast. Note what works for you and write dov why. Describing the experiences is an essential part of learning.

Explore beyond niceness –

look for jazz, blues, opera and rock 'n roll. Wine, like music, is produced in huge variety of styles to suit different moods. The following chart will he you identify what's an easy wine and what's a challenging one. The EAS will provide comfort and the CHALLENGING keeps us stimulated. Challengir wines are usually the better food partner because they create a keen appetite.

Focus on the MEDIUM category of wines first

and develop a repertoire of these. They are the best everyday drinks and most needs. **Then practice having a FRESH wine beforehand or a RIC wine afterwards.** Work on getting a feeling for these three categori and how to use them. Having this kind of structure makes wine learning easy and fast.

Along the way be sure to meet Cabernet,

the Emperor of red wine. Red wine is dominated by the Cabernet grape [and his cousin Merlot] and these wines exude power. At their best they are majestic, but they are far more likely to be merely self-important and serious. **Also seek out the charming, all-American, blonde bombshell, Chardonnay.** Often she's too cute or giddy, but occasionally she has a flash of sincerity and amazing sex appeal. You'll want at least a few dates. While the novice is advised to get acquainted with these two characters, you may eventually seek out reds that are more fun, and whites that are less pretty.

EASY WHITES	CHALLENGING WHITES
Chardonnay	Dry Riesling
Gewurztraminer	Sauvignon Blanc
Pinot Gris	Semillon
Most hot climate whites	Most European whites
EASY REDS	**CHALLENGING REDS**
Shiraz	Bordeaux
Beaujolais	Chianti
Valpolicella Ripasso	some Cabernets
Rioja, and other Spanish reds	Baco Noir
Most hot climate reds	Most European reds

important service details

3 steps to success

quantity **How many bottles should you buy for a party?**

The LCBO suggests 'up to half a bottle per person.' That's a bit stingy. I cannot see a party getting off the ground on that quantity. Father Farrar Capon, an American Episcopal priest and author of many books on theology and gastronomy, decrees "One bottle per person must always be your rule, otherwise your party will end with a whimper instead of a bang. The worst parties I have attended have invariably been those at which the host, out of ignorance or principle [one is as bad as the other], provided a mere two bottles of wine for six people."

P.S. Remember you are responsible if your guests drive home drunk.

glassware **The appropriate glassware does a lot for wine.**

Your enjoyment of red wine is guaranteed to increase if you invest in a few big – the bigger the better – wine goblets. Check out the Riedel line, and if that's too expensive, look for something cheaper but similar in size and feel. You might feel self conscious drinking from a big glass but the pleasure of the wine will quickly cure that. For white wine, I'm very happy with a tall, slender tumbler. It seems to echo the freshness of the wine. The worst glasses in the world are the dinky things that they give you at wine shows. They seem to make the wine unhappy.

temperature colder is cooler

Everyone knows that white wines taste best cold, but red wines also need a degree of chilling. As a rough guide, I give nearly all my reds ten minutes in the freezer. That's right, the freezer. It's fast and won't damage the wine. Reds taste brighter, livelier and more exciting when they are slightly cool, at 'cellar temperature'. Discover this for yourself – you won't believe the difference in taste.

wine serving temperatures

20C		sweet reds	rich reds
18C			
16C			medium reds
14C	rich chardonnays		
12C	medium whites		light reds
10C		rosé	
8 C	light whites		sweet whites
6 C		sparkling	
4C			

S. If you still don't believe in the need to lightly chill most reds, try this test. Pour a ass of tap water without letting it run first. Let the water run a while and fill a second ass. Now taste both. The first will be at room temperature and will taste flat and unap-etizing. The second glass of 'cool' water will be much livelier – it will have vitality.

the good host

a few do's and don'ts

A glass please.

Lovely home, good food, interesting company, lots of open wines but not a glass to be seen. Don let your guests start their evening off badly. Get a clean, decent quality wine glass into yo guest's hands within 10 seconds of arrival. Why not put out a tray of glasses and keep it stocke

Don't overfill.

A full glass of wine robs the the drinker of enticing fragrances and is as unappet ing as food filled too high on a plate. Wine is best enjoyed an inch at a time.

Out of the dark.

Wine, like food, is more appetizing when brightly lit. A well-lit setting makes wine and food fe more flavourful.

Stinky glasses.

Detergent leaves an unpleasant smell in glassware that can be difficult to get r of. It helps if you do not stack glasses upside down and if you rotate them instead always taking them from the front row. Best solution of all is to 'prime' your glass with half an ounce of wine. Priming simply means coating the inside of the glass wi a trace of wine. You may use the same splash of wine for your partner's glass, the chuck the wine.

Don't play it safe.

ear it all the time, "...this wine won't offend anyone." Wimpy wine does offend because it's oring, and if you're not offering excitement what kind of a host are you? We live in a golden age f wine, why not enjoy it?

Good presentation.

Have you ever noticed how a display of wine bottles at the entrance of a restaurant seems to excite the senses? Adopt the idea when entertaining. For dinner parties, have the aperitif wine on ice beside the glassware, ready to pour. Place dinner reds [opened, without the cork] on a sideboard to catch the eye.

Good preparation.

hilling wine, cleaning glassware, opening bottles, etc. takes more time than we think. Start well head. Water added to ice will speed up the chilling.

Not just rich.

Too much rich wine tires the senses and exhausts the body. Always include brisk wines at your events and save the 'couch wines' till near the end.

Penny pinching.

e thrifty for your everyday needs, but when entertaining your friends don't be afraid to break at ten dollar barrier. It does get noticed.

wine talk

The traditional way to taste wine is to analyze the components and repo on the findings. This is not much different from the way works of art, or res aurant meals are reviewed. While this method does help establish variou aspects of the experience, it seldom results in taking you to the heart the matter.

A better way to grasp the essence of something is to look at the bigger pictur Over years of tasting I've been drawn to a direct approach which consists jumping into the middle of things. I've found that if you start on the outsid you often cannot get to the heart, and this is where you want to be. Some the best descriptions of wine have come from people who could not analyz a wine to save their lives. They simply give an honest response to an exper ence just as someone would give to a Rolling Stones concert. Or, as Matiss said, they 'observed . . . and felt the innermost nature of the experience Many people have difficulty doing this with wine because they believe the is a proper wine language and a correct response to each wine. They fear gi ing the wrong answer.

If a wine feels happy, comforting, or dreary, go ahead and say so. There are more mear ingful expressions than what the experts come up with. And your friends will know wh you mean.

"I do not want to deconstruct the pleasure of wine by trying to work out whether the aromas smell of banan or apricots. If you analyze too much, you end up destroying the pleasure..."
Lionel Poilane [France's most famous baker]

ɔad thoughts!!!

ɴly one!? wine

When people tell me they have a favourite wine and it's the only one they buy, I'm astounded. To drink only one wine is like listening to only one song – over and over. Wine, like music, is made in a huge variety of styles to suit every mood and occasion. Develop a repertoire and you'll have way more fun.

our favourite is not! always the best choice

Different occasions call for different wines. It's not OK to serve your favourite wine on every occasion. One hot summer evening I was pouring wine at a reception and a woman asked me if I had a Rioja. She went to great lengths to tell me how much she loved Rioja and I concurred that it was a delicious wine, but 'try a glass of Vinho Verde'. Five minutes later she returned to say 'that was just what I needed'. She thought she wanted Rioja, but what she NEEDED was a refreshing wine. When you have learned to match wine to mood, you will have lots of favourites.

tocking a cellar full of fancy wine can be an interesting obby, but!

If you talk to anyone who's done it they will usually admit that they seldom find occasions to drink the special wines they have collected. "It never seems to be appropriate. A better practice is to invest in good wine for your daily needs. Drink something you really like more often. Live for today.

billy's 10 commandments

for wine enjoyment

1. **Exercise daily.** Make wine a daily companion. With so much to enjoy you'll never make a dent in it unless you drink it everyday.

2. **It's the trip that counts.** Enjoy the good, and keep learning from what you don't like. Tomorrow you'll have different tastes. It will always be a bit confusing, a bit challengin – just like life. That's the excitement. Forget expertise. Bask in the delight.

3. **Chart your own course.** Wine pleasure is as personal as music pleasure. Would you buy all the same CDs as your neighbour? Build your own repertoire of wine wisdom. Indul in your own fancies and frolics. Look for wines that fit nicely into your life.

4. **Find a mentor.** Learning about wine is a process of experiencing and questioning. Every bottle brings up a series of questions – that's why you need a buddy who can supply some answers.

5. **Avoid prestige wine** – and the mob that follow it. Wine, unfortunately, attracts a lot of geeks – people who become obsessed with it and separate the subject from life. They start to speak a language that's not understood by the layman. They aren't having fun and you'll learn nothing from their game – except how to waste money.

6 ■ **Select wines for the moment, the mood.** Make the question 'What wine would be great for right now?' your guiding light. It's matching wine to mood/event that makes the best times, not the price of the bottle.

7 ■ **The communion between people and wine is feeling.** Put aside conventional belief that wine's statement is flavour. The essence or character of a wine can only be felt. It's the feeling that connects wine to our moods and events.

8 ■ There is always too much to choose from so **you need to divide wine into categories such as the ones in this handbook.** When you taste a wine you like, give it a category and then you will remember it more easily.

9 ■ **You need a reference point.** A wine that makes a statement about your likes. For me it's everyday Chianti, the wine with the worker's hands, the wine that most clearly expresses the joy and the struggle of life, the wine that's both appetizing and nourishing. The nature in the wine echoes the lively, colourful nature of a pizza or a bowl of pasta with tomato sauce.

10 ■ **Play your part.** Wine, like music, is interactive. Work on bringing out the best in the wine you open. Set the stage. Create the experience.

food+wine

andy to know

appy couples

general guide

ps

reating flow

season

happy couples

food + wine

Here are some first steps in food and wine pairing. As you'll see, they are all linked b mood, which is why I encourage you to find the mood of each wine you drink so yo can recall it to partner a food or situation.

light 'n bright food+light 'n bright wine

a summer salad, such as Nicoise, with **VINHO VERDE**

brisk food+brisk wine

pizza or colourful antipasto with **BARBERA**

bland food+spicy wine

egg dishes with **DRY MUSCAT**

sweet food+tangy/salty wine

BBQ'd shrimp appetizer with **FINO SHERRY**

charming food+charming wine

grilled salmon with **BEAUJOLAIS**

rich food+rich wine

BBQ'd seafood with **AUSSIE CHARDONNAY**

nappy couples

ood + wine

oily food+tart wine

noked salmon with **ONTARIO DRY RIESLING**

exotic food+exotic wine

oroccan couscous with **PINOT NOIR**

soft, easy food+perky wine

mburger with **BACO NOIR**

macho food+macho wine

illed steak with **CABERNET SAUVIGNON**

comforting food+soul satisfying wine

ast chicken with **CÔTES du RHÔNE**

tangy food+tangy wine

sta in tomato sauce with young **CHIANTI**

plain food+fruity wine

rk or chicken with **BEAUJOLAIS/GAMAY**

matching food + wine

a general guide

appetizers **antipasto** **oysters** **sole** **snapper** **grilled vegetables** **cold cuts** **fresh cheeses** **quiche**	**FRESH WHITES** SOAVE, FRASCATI, SAUVIGNON BLANC, PINOT GRIGIO, PINOT BLANC, ALIGOTÉ, AUXERROIS, VINHO VERDE, RIESLING DRY [Ontario], CHENIN BLANC, GAVI, ORVIETO, CHARDONNAY [Italy] **MEDIUM LIVELY REDS** *lightly chilled* VALPOLICELLA, BARBERA, MONTEPULCIANO D'ABRUZZO, CÔTES DU RHÔNE, CÔTES DU LUBERON, CÔTES DU VENTOUX, BEAUJOLAIS, GAMAY [Ontario], DRY ROSÉ
pasta tomato sauce **pizza** **risotto** **grilled salmon** **bruschetta** **quesadilla**	**MEDIUM LIVELY REDS** *lightly chilled* VALPOLICELLA, BARBERA, CHIANTI [not Riserva], MONTEPULCIANO D'ABRUZZO, CÔTES DU RHÔNE, CÔTES DU LUBERON, CÔTES DU VENTOUX, BEAUJOLAIS, GAMAY [Ontario], CABERNET FRANC [under $12, Ontario]
Tex Mex **Asian** **Cajun** **burgers + ribs** with ketchup/sauce **beans** **samosas**	**MEDIUM WHITES and MEDIUM REDS** PINOT NOIR [under $15], ZINFANDEL [under $15], SHIRAZ [under $15], MERLOT [under $15, hot climate], BACO NOIR [Ontario], RIOJA [under $15], CHARDONNAY [Chile, Australia], DRY ROSÉ

atching food + wine

general guide

icken **al, pork** **rkey, game** **lmon, tuna** **vordfish, lasagna** **oussaka**	**MEDIUM REDS** CRU BEAUJOLAIS, GAMAY, CÔTES DU RHÔNE-VILLAGES, PINOT NOIR [Oregon, California, Ontario], RIOJA [under $15], AUSSIE SHIRAZ [under $15], VALPOLICELLA RIPASSO, DAO, MERLOT [under $15], ZINFANDEL [under $15], RHONE STYLE [from California], CABERNET FRANC [Ontario], DRY ROSÉ
ılmon, **ırimp, lobster** **rab, grouper** **ɔast pork** **aked ham** **asta** cream sauce **hite meat** creamsauce	**RICH WHITES** CHARDONNAY [over $12, Ontario, California, Australia, Chile, South Africa], WHITE BURGUNDY, POUILLY FUMÉ, SANCERRE, SAUVIGNON BLANC or FUMÉ BLANC [over $12, California, New Zealand, Chile], SEMILLON [Australia], PINOT GRIS [Alsace], WHITE RIOJA [over $12]
eef or lamb rilled or roasted	**RICH REDS** BORDEAUX, CABERNET and MERLOT [over $15, from anywhere], AUSSIE SHIRAZ [over $15], CHATEAUNEUF DU PAPE, CHIANTI RISERVA, RIOJA RESERVA, DAO, ZINFANDEL

e principle is to pair wines and foods of somewhat similar personalities/moods – hthearted with lighthearted, nourishing with nourishing, fancy with fancy, etc. This ide is based on wines that are generally available at our liquor stores.

food + wine tips

off to a good start

The first wine you serve at dinner, at a party, or even on a picnic, should be novel. A possible new experience for your guests. People are open to novelty at the beginning – they want a surprise. They know that you're going to give them something nice later. A simple way to provide novelty in the summer months is to start with a chilled lively red. Give 'em Chardonnay later.

the BBQ

Lively, fruity and cheerful wines work best with BBQ'd foods and moods. It's best if they have a sweet impression because that's a good contrast with the charred flavours. Hot climate SHIRAZ, MERLOT or PINOT NOIR are good choices with red meat. CÔTES DU RHÔNE and BEAUJOLAIS are my favourite wines with white meats.

Fans of white wine cannot go wrong with rich CHARDONNAY.

my summer bucket of refreshment

Put four to s bottles of my 'FRESH', 'Dry Rosé', a 'MEDIUM LIVELY RED' selections in a buc et of iced water and you have an insta portable, summer wine bar. Let friends all the wines by pouring just a few ounc at a time. Different moods and situatio will cause certain wines to work bett than others. Keep the whites and rosés w chilled, and the reds lightly chilled.

wine for chocolate

Buy some far truffles, arrange them nicely on a pla and serve with a chilled glass of Framboi eavenly. SOUTHBROOK FARMS FRAM- OISE, Ontario [#341024 375ml/$15.45]

ines with you your sweetie on

valentine's

PER-HEIDSIECK Champagne, with the pret- red label, would be my choice for a alentine celebration. Diamond-Cut Toasts ith Roses of Smoked Salmon are a possible ibbly with the bubbly. A seafood wine for inner could be CAVE SPRING RESERVE RIES- NG partnered with a Love Boat of Oysters, lams and Shrimp. Next, serve Roasted oves with Fresh Lovage and the red wine of vers, PINOT NOIR from FETZER. A dessert of hocolate Soufflé with Napoleons and sephines could accompany SOUTHBROOK RMS FRAMBOISE. Hope this is not too much ouble!

ines with you your sweetie in

summer

In Italy, carna- ons are a powerful symbol of love and, dded to wine, were long believed to have an hrodisiac quality. Secure one bottle of illed ASTI SPUMANTE and nine deep red rnations in the morning. Wash the carnations. Drink a glass of the wine [to make room for the carnations] and push the petals into the bottle and recork with a champagne stopper, or let the handle of a silver teaspoon dangle into the bottle. Return the wine to the refrigerator for 4 – 6 hours. Serve to your loved one, petals and all.

wines with you your sweetie in

winter

Add a tablespoon of fresh or dried jasmine flowers to mulled wine and pour unstrained. Dab a little jasmine oil at your partner's throat. Sip and neck.

will that be

stressed or carefree?

Anxiety and stress are pushing more and more people towards the rich, comfort style of wine and food. Merlot and steak. Those who can still manage a carefree mood are likely to indulge in more festive, experimental or exotic wines and foods. Maybe Mexican with Zinfandel, or Thai with Riesling.

creating flow

give a great dinner party

A dinner party has its flow and each drink should contribute the right energy at the right moment. Each of the moods throughout the evening requires a different wine.

aperitif rev up with a glass of Ontario Dry Riesling.

Cranks up the senses + energizes.

antipasto appetizer get in gear with a spirited Gamay or Barbera.

Light reds are fun. They put you in the party mood. Serve lightly chilled.

seafood course cruise for a while with a flashy Chardonnay.

The party is gathering momentum and it needs a high-octane, sunshine wine like Chardonnay. Something expressive, and glamorous.

meat course rendezvous with a handsome Chianti, Cabernet, Ripasso or Syrah.

You're now ready for the nourishing qualities of a substantial red wine.

dessert park and cuddle up with a sweetie, such as a Select Late-Harvest Vidal.

Sweetness and charm are the ingredients needed now. A nightcap of rich, sexy flavours.

[d]rinking in season

[f]ood + wine

[Th]e seasons contribute a lot to our moods and the following are a few [dr]inking ideas that you may like to explore.

spring

In of the first warm days of April or May, I like to take a bottle of **Sauvignon Blanc** out into the garden I pour myself a big glass – and I taste **Spring**.

summer

With **Vinho Verde** and **Gamay** in my ice bucket, **every Summer day is perfect**

fall

I greet falling leaves and falling temperatures with the red wines that are on the beginning of the rich curve.

Roast chicken with Chardonnay, or grilled salmon with Beaujolais, taste good any day of the year.

winter

Hearty local **Baco** or Italy's **Ripasso** offer the rustic character that gladdens and warms the **heart** in the **icy Winter months.**

buying wine

LCBO

private wine stores

LCBO vintages

at the wineries

Beamsville

Niagara-on-the-Lake

the Southwest

Toronto

wine events calender

buying wine at the LCBO

the seven biggies There are seven stores that stock all LCBO wines:

- ☐ Queen's Quay & Cooper Street, Toronto 416.864.6777
- ☐ Crossroads, Weston Road & Hwy. 401, Toronto 416.243.3320
- ☐ Bayview & Sheppard Avenues, Toronto 416.222.7658
- ☐ 409 Highland Road, Kitchener 519.745.8781
- ☐ 71 York Street, London 519.432.1831
- ☐ 1980 Bank Street, Ottawa 613.523.7763
- ☐ 3155 Howard Avenue, Windsor 519.967.1772
- **NEW!** ☐ 1123 Yonge Street, Toronto 416.922.2924
  Opening early 2003 at the restored Summerhill Railway station

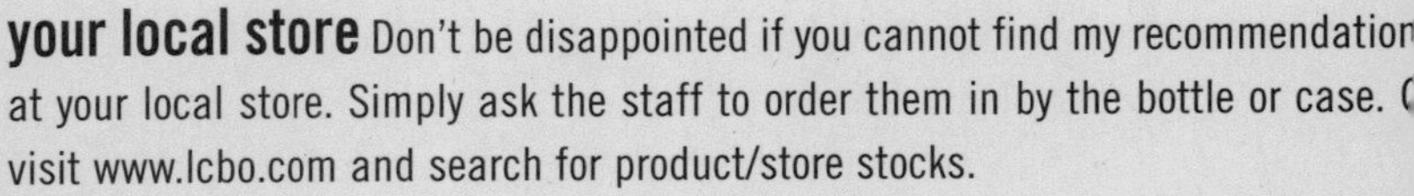

your local store Don't be disappointed if you cannot find my recommendatio at your local store. Simply ask the staff to order them in by the bottle or case. visit www.lcbo.com and search for product/store stocks.

LCBO info line You can get information on wine availability at any store by cal ing the LCBO Infoline. In Toronto, call 416.365.5900. Elsewhere you can call toll-fr at 1.800.ONT.LCBO. The lines are open 9 a.m. to 6 p.m., Monday to Saturday.

price changes A reader asked why wine prices change so often. Because wir is produced by thousands of individuals under different conditions in thousands different parts of the world, its price will tend to fluctuate more than the price toothpaste. Prices given in BILLY'S BEST BOTTLES HANDBOOK are those at pres time, but expect some of them to have changed by the time you shop.

ɔuying at the supermarkets

ɪe Wine Rack, The Wine Shoppe, and Colio Wine Boutiques [located mainly in super-
arkets] are worth visiting because they offer a few excellent wines not available at
:BOs. Call for the locations nearest to you.

THE WINE RACK [INNISKILLIN, JACKSON-TRIGGS and SAWMILL CREEK]

ɴISKILLIN 99 PINOT NOIR RESERVE $16.95

ɴISKILLIN 99 CABERNET FRANC RESERVE $18.95

ɪns of mature reds should not miss this pair of delicious winter warmers.
gh quality wines at reasonable prices. 1.800.265.9463 www.winerack.com

THE WINE SHOPPE
ILLEBRAND and PELLER ESTATES]

.LEBRAND VINEYARD SELECT 2001 PINOT BLANC $9.95

.LEBRAND VINEYARD SELECT 2001 SAUVIGNON BLANC $9.25

LLER ESTATES 2000 DRY RIESLING 'PRIVATE RESERVE' $14.95

llebrand's Pinot Blanc is a charmer with the ideal personality for house wine. Sip any-
ne. The Sauvignon Blanc is a wonderful expression of this grape. An early evening or
ırty drink. Peller's Riesling is a classy aperitif or partner for fish or fowl.
800.230.4321 www.winecountryathome.com

COLIO WINE BOUTIQUES

ılio Estates Vineyards [CEV] wines have generous flavours and great drinkability.
ith fowl, try the spicy 1999 CABERNET FRANC [$19.95].
800.265.1322 or 519.738.2241

LCBO vintages stores

The board created this separate division to sell drinks that were not available in th quantities necessary to supply its six hundred LCBO stores. Vintages stores operate li a market in that new wines arrive on the shelves twice a month and when they're sol they're gone. The ratio of good to boring wines is about the same at Vintages as at re ular LCBOs – one in ten. Their beautiful monthly catalogue tries hard to ma you believe otherwise. I should point out that all the comments in my Handbook refer regular LCBO wines and not to any Vintages items. While one can get along quite nice without Vintages wine, I recommend it to anyone with the enthusiasm for more variet

There are two Vintages stores in Toronto, one in Mississauga and one in Ottawa. All th bigger LCBOs carry a selection of Vintages wines.

tips on shopping at

Hot items sell out quickly at the main stores. A regular LCBO wi a Vintages section is often your best bet. Sure, it may not have the f selection, but you can at least get a portion of what you're after.

Don't admit defeat right away. Some clerks take delight in saying 'a gone' when, in fact, there may be lots of stock at other stores. Use th LCBO INFO-LINE, 1.800.ONT.LCBO [416.365.5900], or the web, for an accu rate stock report.

Most important tip – do not attempt to shop the Vintages department without inside help. The Board has spent a fortune training Product Consultants who are there to help you. Find a good one and you'll be amazed by how hard they'll work to locate wines for you. Wine is not like Corn Flakes, you need 'contacts' to secure some bottles. And remember that good old-fashioned hugs, kisses and thank yous are what make the world come your way.

Be willing to admit defeat occasionally. And don't worry. The world is producing more good wine than ever and I'll guarantee that today's missed great bottles will be replaced by equally good ones tomorrow.

ocations

Toronto
- ☐ Queen's Quay & Cooper Street 416.864.6777
- ☐ 2901 Bayview Avenue, Bayview Village Mall 416.222.7658

Mississauga
- ☐ 1900 Dundas Street West, Sherwood Forrest Mall 905.823.4524

Ottawa
- ☐ 275 Rideau Street 613.789.5226

;. Vintages also publishes a catalogue of 'classic' wines starting around $15. Just about all the great drinks the world [including Cognac, Scotch, Port, etc.] are offered. Older bottles and large format bottles make eat gifts. You can order by phone, have your order shipped to your local store and pay by credit card. Pick the catalogue at any LCBO that has a Vintages section.

www.wineroute.com

local wine tours

Niagara

If you are not familiar with the Niagara region I'd like to point out that there are tw distinct wine areas; the **BEAMSVILLE BENCH**, which is west of St. Catharines, an **NIAGARA-ON-THE-LAKE**, which is at the tip of the Peninsula. It's best to choose ju one area unless you are spending a few days. Beamsville would be my first choic because it has better views from the Escarpment, but nobody should miss seeing th new Jackson-Triggs winery which is close to Niagara-on-the-Lake.

eamsville area

om Grimsby to Jordan along regional road #81

eninsula ridge estates [Regional Road 81, Grimsby] Spectacular storation of an estate farm. High-end wines and a high-end restaurant. A showpiece.)5.563.0900

alivoire winery [Regional Road 81, Beamsville] Tasteful high-end winery. stinctive, concentrated, rich wines. Open weekends or by appointment. 905.563.9253

astdell estates [4041 Locust Lane, Beamsville] Good everyday wines. Very pular destination because of its casualness and the views from the café/restaurant. els like you're visiting someone's cottage. 905.563.WINE

ineland estates [3620 Meyer Road, Vineland] Niagara's best located win- y. You're bound to be impressed. Lunch on the huge deck. Dinner at the restaurant. esling for ageing is still the speciality, but now Chardonnay, Sauvignon Blanc, Pinot is, Gewurztraminer and Cabernet are stars too. 905.562.7088

ave spring cellars [Main Street, Jordan] Good taste in everything, includ- g the huge restaurant and deluxe accommodation across the street. A great show- ece. Lunch here, perhaps, or have an early dinner at the end of the day. Or just a cold er. Make Cave Spring your touring base. Top-rated Chardonnay, Riesling, Auxerrois, abernet and Gamay. A full service winery for sure. 905.562.3581

continued

Beamsville area

local wine tours continued . . .

henry of pelham [1469 Pelham Road] Former coaching inn. Cozy, friendly, p atmosphere here. Picnic area and snack bar. Traditional, hands-on family winery with talented winemaker. May be Niagara's top winery right now. Chardonnay, Rieslin Sauvignon Blanc, Baco Noir, Cabernet and Merlot. And a fantastic Brut Sparkli 'Cuvee Catharine'. 905.684.8423

creekside estates [2170 Fourth Avenue, Jordan Station] Not much to lo at, but a young Aussie winemaker is doing great things with Sauvignon Blanc, Riesli and Pinot Noir. Highend. 905.562.0033

13th street wine co. [3983 13th Street, Jordan Station] Two small wine ies in one: G.H. FUNK and SANDSTONE. Very high quality wines, especially Rieslin Gamay and Pinot Noir. Open Saturdays only. 905.562.9463

ıagara-on-the-Lake area

ocal wine tours continued . . .

ıllebrand winery [Highway 55, Virgil] Big place, can be busy, with tastings nd tours conducted by well-trained staff. Great range of wines with quality at all lev-ls. Large restaurant – one of the best in Niagara. Patio overlooking vineyards. Tons of vents. 905.468.7123 or 1.800.582.8412

ackson-triggs [Highway 55, Niagara-on-the-Lake] Modern spin on the tra-itional barn design. Fantastic space for the production of wine, for tasting it, and for njoying the vineyard vistas. A refreshing break from *ye olde* look. Take a tour and check ut the outdoor amphitheatre. Excellent mid-range and everyday wines, many recom ended in this book. 905.468.4637

eller estates [290 John Street, Niagara-on-the-Lake] Chateaux grandeur in eeping with historic homes on the same street. Very much the country manor, complete ith elegant restaurant overlooking the vineyards. A lovely lunch stop. Patio too. One of e smartest tasting rooms in Niagara. Full range of wines, from charming 'Private eserve' 2000 Riesling [$12], right up to the impressive 'Signature Series' 1999 Cabernet auvignon [$44]. 905.468.4678

trewn winery [1339 Lake Shore Road, Niagara-on-the-Lake] Nice grounds nd good mix of modern and old in this former canning factory. Fantastic Dry Riesling ith several past years still available. Good Cabernet Franc too. The on-site *La Cachette* staurant serves quality French Bistro food and feels quite relaxing compared to places town. There is a cooking school too. 905.468.1229 www.strewnwinery.com

the southwest – Lake Erie North Shore

local wine tours continued . . .

This is Canada's most southerly vineyard district. It stretches between Leamingto and Amherstburg, but it is best known for Pelee Island. It enjoys a 2 to 3 week longe growing season than Niagara and if you're planning a mid-summer visit be prepare for very hot weather.

d'angelo winery [5th Concession, RR#4 Amherstburg] Home of Sal D'Angel one of the original growers in the region. Full range of wines, with Marechal Foch ofte being the showstopper. 519.736.7959

leblanc winery [4716 Concession 4, Harrow] Lyse Leblanc tends a sheltere inland vineyard and her wines have a delicate, pure quality. Packaged in hand-dec rated bottles. 519.738.9228

grape tree estates [308 Mersea Road 3, Leamington] New kid on th block, Steve Brook, is a former LCBO product consultant. Now he's running two vine yards and producing some of the most interesting wines in the region, including a tas sparkler, 'Hexagon', made from six grapes. Steve is enthusiastic about the wines, th food, the culture and just about everything else in his region. Visit him. Future plan include a B&B and a restaurant. 519.322.2081

continu

he southwest – Lake Erie North Shore

cal wine tours continued . . .

olio estates winery [1 Colio Drive, Harrow] has an attractive revamped nery and tasting room. The quality and value of Colio's everyday wines is one of the asons I drink local wine. Winemaker Carlo Negri works a 'good drinkability' spirit into erything he produces. Try his Cabernet Franc. 519.738.224

elee island winery [455 Seacliff, County Road 20, Kingsville] Reasonably iced, good everyday wines in attractive packaging have made Pelee one of e most successful wineries in Canada. The 'Vinedresser Series', a new line premium wines, should prove to be another feather in their cap. The winery on the mainland but there is a Wine Pavilion on the island offer g food, entertainment and drink. It's a two hour ferry ride. 9.724.2469 www.peleeisland.com

Toronto's wineland

local wine tours continued . . .

All four of Toronto's wineries are located close to each other in the northeast cor ner of the city, which goes by various names such as Vaughan, Woodbridge ar Maple. Maybe they will simplify it one day and just call the area 'Wineland'. All a open Sundays as is the café/shop mentioned at the end. The following is a rundov of what to expect when you visit.

magnotta winery Magnotta is developing a following with its plan to b come an alternative to the LCBO. A huge range of drinks is offered at prices ten to twe ty percent lower than the LCBO's. Magnotta's ICEWINE, in a distinctive blue bottle, se for considerably less than that of other wineries. Magnotta's headquarters are as b and wonderful as a New York art gallery – and so unexpected in this discount warehou suburb of T.O.. A winegarden is open in summer, and the huge cellars beneath the sto are available for private functions. Call for the locations of other stores.
271 Chrislea Road, Woodbridge 905.738.WINE or 1.800.461.9463

southbrook farms Southbrook's Bill Redelmeier and partners are having f producing local versions of Burgundy and Bordeaux in old farm buildings just north Toronto. Framboise has been the big success to date, but Chardonnay, Sauvignon Blar Pinot Noir and Cabernet have hit high spots too. Many wine events are held during t summer. Southbrook also has a huge roadside produce shop.
1061 Major Mackenzie Drive, Richmond Hill 905.832.2548

continu

'oronto's wineland

ɔcal wine tours continued . . .

ˈinotecca winery Giovanni and Rosanna Follegot, of Vinoteca Winery, are ˈodels of old-world humility. They see themselves as a winery for the family, making ˈine at prices people want to pay – lots of everyday wines, some wine for celebrations ˈnd a little fancy stuff. They sell Niagara/Italy blends for $6.95. Chardonnay and Cab-ˈnet sold under the RESERVE label are rich, ripe and flavourful.
27 Jevlan Drive, Woodbridge 905.856.5700

ilento winery Like its neighbours, Cilento grew out of the juice-for-wine usiness. Thirty acres have been planted in Niagara and this ultra-smart winery dis-ˈays a serious commitment to local wine. Best wines so far have been RIESLING [out :anding], CABERNET FRANC and a LATE HARVEST VIDAL.
27 Chrislea Road, Woodbridge 905.856.3874

S. If you'd like to add a little food and fashion to your trip, step ˈto the huge, disco-like clothing shop called Motor Oil. Very ɔorty. Everyone needs a new pair of jeans. Part of the shop is a :ylish, arty 'cool Italian' café called Americani.

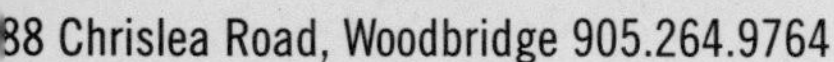
88 Chrislea Road, Woodbridge 905.264.9764

wine events calendar

×january×february

Pacific Northwest Wine Fair at Roy Thompson Hall, Toronto 416.410.4630
Guelph Wine Gala 519.821.7570
Niagara's Days of Wine & Roses 905.468.4263

×march

Ontario's Cuvée Niagara-on-the-Lake 1.800.361.6645
Toronto Wine & Cheese Show 416.229.2060 or 1.800.896.7469

×april

Vancouver Playhouse International Wine Fest 604.873.3311
The Toronto Hospital Wine Classic 416.340.3935
Burlington Wine and Food Expo 905.634.7736

×may

Santé: Bloor-Yorkville Wine Festival 416.928.3555 ext.24 www.santewinefestival.net
California Wine Fair 1.800.558.2675 Ottawa & Toronto
Wine & Food 'Tastings' 519.485.5321 Elmhurst Inn, Ingersoll

×june

Apple Blossom Fruit Wine & Food Festival at Archibald Orchards & Winery, Bowmanville 905.263.2396
Southwestern Ontario Food & Wine Extravaganza at Bellemere Winery, London 519.473.2273
Theatre Aquarius Vine Dining in Hamilton 905.522.7529 or 1.800.465.7529
Toronto Taste 416.408.2594

ıeatre Beyond Words: Wine Auction Niagara-on-the-Lake 1.800.268.5774
ew Vintage Niagara Celebrations: Gala Wine Tasting and Winery Passports
)5.688.1212 www.grapeandwine.com

julyxaugust

illebrand's Annual Jazz & Blues Festivals, Niagara 905.468.7123
iagara's Unforgettable Vineyard Weekends 416.777.6342 or 905.684.8070
stival Du Vin Des Laurentides 1.800.363.7777
sta Buckhorn at Buckhorn Community Centre [near Peterborough] 705.657.8833
nger Lakes Grassroots Festival 607.378.5098

september

ıtario Wine Festival at Southbrook Farms, Toronto 905.832.2458
agara Grape and Wine Festival, St. Catharines 905.688.0212 or 416.777.6342
ast of Fields Food and Wine Picnic 905.859.3609
ste of Sault Ste. Marie 705.946.2503

octoberxnovemberxdecember

kanagan Wine Festival in Penticton, B.C. 604.860.5999
orth Bay Wine Gala, Capital Centre 705.474.1944
tawa Art Gallery Wine Auction 613.233.8699
under Bay 'Wine Affair' 807.684.4444
tawa Wine & Food Show 613.567.6408
ronto Symphony Wine Auction & Tastings 416.593.7769
stralian Wine Fair in Toronto 416.323.3909 ext. 303
nhos De Espana at Great Hall of Hart House, U of Toronto 416.979.3353 ext. 380
ronto Gourmet Food + Wine Show Expo 416 410 0405 www.foodandwineshow.ca
rts of Wine Festival, Halifax 1.800.567.5874
cce, Novello + Noodles [my bash] 416.530.1545 www.billysbestbottles.com

WARNING

The wine business moves so fast that anything you think you know is already no longer valid. The new stuff keeps streaming down. More than half of what you've read in this handbook is sure to be invalid by the end of 2003.

PLEASE DESTROY

this book at year's end and get the new edition. It will do us both good. Contact info@billysbestbottles.com to order the 2004 edition.

If you enjoyed this book please buy a copy for a friend.

It will do us all good.

want more? we have more! . . . for the enthusiast!

If you have enjoyed this book, chances are you'll also enjoy my BEST BOTTLES WINELETTER. It comes out every other month and contains 40 pages of reviews – good and bad – of all the new wines as they arrive at the LCBO. Each issue is jammed with dozens of hot tips, lots of useful information and wine chat. You'll also find a smattering of my restaurant and bar selections and occasional beer reviews. The best buys from LCBO Vintages Stores are also offered along with a handy shopping list and the issue's best picks wine cards. BEST BOTTLES is in it's 20th year, surviving on the support of subscribers – and no advertising dollars. I'd be glad to send you a complimentary copy to check out before you subscribe.

See the other side for details.

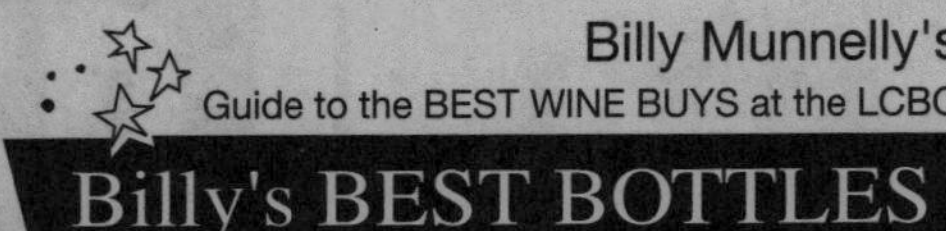

helping people buy and understand wine

SEND ME

Billy's Best Bottles Wineletter

☐ a **2 year** subscription $86
[12 issues ~ includes 7% GST] **save $10**

☐ a **1 year** subscription $48
[6 issues ~ includes 7% GST]

name ________________________

address ________________________

____

____________ code ____________

email ________________________

new subscription ☐

gift subscription ☐ from ________________________

message on gift card ________________________

____

method of payment:
cheque enclosed ☐ visa ☐ mastercard ☐

card # ________________________

expiration date ________________________

name on card ________________________

"You do a fantastic job and I raise my glass to those who know how to live well!"

S. Pope, Ottawa

"Love your caustic comments, your wacky art direction and your anti-snobbery perspective – please renew my subscription!"

K. Hagan, Toronto

"Instead of buying blindly I now know what to expect."

J. Sanders, Toronto

"Thank you for providing such great information and witticisms. I am kept simultaneously amused and inebriated. . . an altogether not unpleasant state to be in."

J.J. Johnson, Etobicoke

"Very readable, not pompous, and even outrageous at times. You bring fun and a fresh perspective to the enjoyment of wine."

H. Haney, Etobicoke

Billy's Best Bottles
589 Markham Street
Toronto Ontario
M6G 2L7

P: 416.530.1545
F: 416.530.1575
E: info@billysbestbottles.com
www.billysbestbottles.com

we experience wine
through our
moods, situations,
thoughts,
imagination and
feelings

billy's best bottles annual wine handbook

billy's best bottles wineletter

wine education + training

hospitality + wine events

restaurant service training

restaurant graphic+design

restaurant winelist construction

wine spectrum tastings

Billy Munnelly + Kato Wake

Billy's Best Bottles
589 Markham Street
Toronto Ontario
M6G 2L7

P: 416.530.1545
F: 416.530.1575
E: info@billysbestbottles.com